Me Now – Who Next?

The Inspiring Story of
a Traumatic Brain Injury Recovery

Angela Leigh Tucker

As Told by **Bill Ramsey**

Me Now – Who Next?
The Inspiring Story of a Traumatic Brain Injury Recovery
by
Angela Leigh Tucker
Bill Ramsey

© Copyright January 2, 2014
Angela Leigh Tucker
Bill Ramsey

ISBN-10: 1492824224
ISBN-13: 978-1492824220

Table of Contents

Introduction

Nothing changes a person's life so completely as an unexpected and sudden health crisis. Brain injuries are at the top of the list. It is likely that you know a brain injury survivor. In fact, whether you realize it or not, you may be one of those survivors.

For those who suffer a brain injury and survive, life is changed. Unlike diseases, traumatic brain injuries have nothing to do with family history and most have little to do with lifestyle choices. Brain injuries occur with no warning; one day well and next day hell! It was certainly that way for Angela Leigh Tucker.

Though millions of people suffer brain injuries, we know very little about these life-altering and often fatal events. The United States Centers for Disease Control and Prevention estimates that at least 1.7 million people sustain a traumatic brain injury each year. They range from mild to severe. Of that number 52,000 die and 275,000 are hospitalized. The remainder go without medical diagnosis or treatment, damaged but able to function. As our ability to recognize and assess brain injuries improves, the number of cases continues to grow.

An unknown number of those who do not seek immediate treatment will die, deaths rarely known to us.

The exceptions are the occasional news report of some celebrity who ran into a tree while skiing, initially said he was fine, declined treatment and died suddenly hours later.

Even with timely treatment, a brain injury may result in long term consequences including vision problems, headaches, diminished sense of taste or smell, ringing in the ears, dizziness, confusion, forgetfulness, cognitive and personality disorders, balance problems and fatigue.

Those spared any serious consequences from the first brain insult may be left susceptible to severe injury in any future concussive event. It is almost as though the brain "remembers" having been injured before. Those who suffer a brain insult or injury must be aware of their personal history and make decisions about how to live their post-injury lives.

There are a variety of ways in which brain function can be interrupted. Each hour of every day, brains are seriously injured in a car crash, contact sport, physical assault, military action or an ordinary fall. These are concussion type injuries. The head comes in contact with an unforgiving surface and the brain is slammed and perhaps spun a little inside the skull. The substantial protection ordinarily afforded by the skull is simply not enough to protect against a heavy blow, and a brain injury results.

Brain damage often occurs without a concussive event. Brain injuries caused by strokes are the second leading killer in the United States. Add to the list oxygen deprivation brain injuries from incidents like near-drowning. Then there are the penetration injuries caused when something pierces the skull and enters the brain as in the case of a bullet wound. Brain tumors are another significant source.

While brain injuries have different causes, they have much in common as to how they impact the lives of those who suffer them. Also, success in recovery from any of the variety of brain injuries calls for many of the same medical procedures and therapies. Even with the selection and use of the best treatments available, a patient may experience an uncertain and less than satisfactory outcome.

How is it that with the overwhelming total number of brain injuries from all causes, the public hears relatively little about them? Why is so little research and treatment money available? Why is the insurance coverage inadequate for those fortunate enough to have insurance coverage? Could it be that brain injury awareness lacks a good public relations program?

For now, we are left with a sense that we know so little about brain injuries, in part, because we allow ourselves to know so little. It may be difficult to imagine ourselves or a loved one having to function in this world with a BRAIN INJURY. Amputation, paralysis, physical disfigurement, blindness, and deafness are challenges that we can discuss with those who have suffered them. We can and do talk about them.

Why is a brain injury so different? Often brain injured persons look like they did before the injury. They seem to act as they did before. Only when we interact closely and repeatedly over a period of days or weeks do we begin to "see" their problem. With protracted exposure we realize that something about them is not what we expected. When this realization kicks in, we may feel uncomfortable and not know how or even whether to proceed. Do we regard those with a brain injury much as we do those with mental illness, another health problem our society avoids?

In spite of progress made in the past ten years, medical science still has much to learn about the brain. Exactly how does it function? How does it heal itself when injured? We do know that it heals, sometimes miraculously, but we also know that the healing cannot be forced upon the brain. A seriously broken bone, when enclosed in a cast, will predictably heal within weeks. Already enclosed in the skull, the brain is inaccessible; no curative splint or cast can be applied. There are no pills or injections available. Surgery, if performed, is usually to relieve pressure or to remove a tumor, bone fragment, bullet or other foreign object. Such surgery is risky and can cause additional damage. Fixing the injured brain is one of medicine's major remaining challenges.

This book is not a medical or scientific treatise on the human brain and the injuries that it may suffer. If after reading Angela Leigh Tucker's story you want to know more on the subject, helpful books and websites are available. We especially recommend their use to those attempting to recovery from a brain injury themselves or for anyone committed to helping with a recovery. Select resources are listed in the Appendix.

As you read of Angela's injury, please keep reminding yourself that it is true and unvarnished. A fictionalized account could be written more quickly and with less need for research and interviews. It would also be much less emotionally demanding because the real pain and suffering that Angela experienced could be avoided or smoothed over. However, a fictional account would not be helpful to others with brain injuries and those who love and support them. The brain injured are in for a tough fight to recover. They need to know what to expect. They need the truth.

The names, places and events shared here are real. Using the names and direct quotes of real people honors those who helped Angela in her struggle to recover. It is important to realize that there are people who stand ready to help in a time of need. Those with injured brains need not be alone in their struggle unless they choose to go it alone.

Angela could not have progressed as well as she has without the love and help of her own "recovery team." There were and still are untold numbers of medical professionals, therapists, family members, friends, co-workers, neighbors and total strangers on her team. If we included all those who inquired about her and prayed for her recovery, the number would run into the thousands.

This is the story of Angela Leigh Tucker who was born on March 21, 1978 and lived a happy, full and successful life until it almost ended on July 31, 2008.

Just after her thirtieth birthday and less than one year into her marriage, she suffered severe physical injuries and a traumatic brain injury in a car crash. Her young husband died instantly at the scene. She wanted her story to be told and I am honored to help her tell it.

1

Preparing for Life

Youth is the time we are given to prepare for life. Angela used that time well. As a result, she was about as prepared as a person could be for what was to befall her. From her earliest days, she dealt with life as it came at her. The divorce of her parents during her childhood was just one blow she experienced. She constructively dealt with challenges and readied herself for life as an adult. Her strength and readiness account for her ability to survive and thrive after her traumatic brain injury.

Reporting on Angela's childhood presents a dilemma. Should we tell the whole story or only those parts that she can remember after the crash? Since the traumatic brain injury occurred, there is much she cannot remember about her youth and the early years of her adult life.

If she were to try telling her whole story she would have to rely heavily on scrap books, journals, yearbooks and photo albums. Her friends and her family would have to tell us about her and what they recall. The result would be a patchwork quilt of her memories and items collected here and there to fill in the blanks.

We decided to rely heavily on the memories she retained after the traumatic brain injury. Reporting only what she recalls means there will be gaps. Some major events will not be reported upon as she simply cannot remember them.

Why did we decide to report that way? We wanted to demonstrate that memory gaps become a part of life for TBI survivors. Is it frustrating for them? Yes! But their frustration only intensifies when those around them somehow expect them to remember everything. Even without a brain injury, none of us can remember everything.

In an attempt to help and reassure her about her recovery, people may ask her to recall moments that she cannot. "Come on, Angela. Surely you remember your having met Maya Angelou and Nelson Mandela?" She cannot recall that although it did happen. Yet some of those who know of her brain injury still seem to expect her to remember many details from the past. Those expectations seem unfair at a minimum and even a little inconsiderate and unkind.

There is a second reason for relying on her personal memories to tell the story. To fill the gaps in her memory by relying upon the memories of others would quickly turn the book into fiction. Using what friends remember of Angela's pre-injury life would result in an imperfect picture at best. If memories were provided for her, how would she accurately know her own past? Better that she fill in the missing pieces herself even if it takes time and leaves gaps. After all, it is her life.

Some friends from childhood and college years were interviewed but not to provide memories that Angela could not. We simply wanted to understand how she had influenced them in her formative years. What had they learned from Angela?

Cheri Cable, now a nurse in Florida, said of her friend: "Angela and I have known each other since fourth grade. We were in Girl Scouts together. We took horseback riding and tennis lessons together. We shared lots of excitement but also had quiet moments together when we would watch for falling stars while rocking on the back porch or listening to leaves rustle while taking a hike. We got into some mischief too. We would steal cookies as my sister baked them. We would jump on the neighbor's trampoline when they were not at home.

"It was easy for us to create our own excitement and scare ourselves while doing it. One night, after watching a scary movie, we heard a "spirit" singing in her room. We hugged each other most of the night before realizing that we had forgotten to turn the radio volume all the way off. We were close as children and still are."

Lance Wafler, another friend from childhood, added perspective about Angela's teen years. "Angela was very involved in a wide range of school activities. She was a member of the tennis team and participated in dramatic productions.

"She was one of these kids who was popular with her friends but equally popular with their parents who felt her influence on their kids was positive. My own parents were among those who really loved her. I have seen my Dad cry only twice in my life. One of those times was more than ten years after our graduation when Dad was told of Angela's crash and her near-fatal injuries.

"Angela and I went on a ten-day chaperoned senior trip to London, Madrid and Paris. We were hooked-up with some kids from a Daytona high school. She immediately became the unofficial voice for the entire group. Many of us wanted to party but Angela would insist that we do something educational. She would make us go to museums and castles, always trying to experience as much as she could."

Here are some observations about Angela's high school years from friend, Tiara Alfrey. "Soon after getting her driver's license, Angela was driving down a rural road when she saw a young mother in a panic; her daughter was choking. Angela pulled off the road, took control of the situation and saved the girl's life. She has always been a take-charge person. Happily, that same little girl was a kindergarten pupil the following school year in the class taught by Angela's mother.

"Angela went to work as a food server in an assisted living facility. She convinced me to take a job there too. I marveled at her ability to make the even the grumpy residents smile.

"She was a good student who was popular with her teachers. Her mom was a teacher and that may have been part of Angela's inspiration. Her academic strength was most evident in English where her creative writing skills could really shine. On the other hand, math was a great challenge for her, perhaps her only weak academic area.

"She was on student council all four years. Although not a cheerleader, she effectively used her charisma to get others fired-up at pep rallies and school sports events. In fact, she was the first non-cheerleader to win the award as Most Spirited Senior. She had a way of making others join the fun, making others feel special. She had a way of leading without showing off or seeking personal attention. She was the single most important reason I wanted to go to school every day."

Another dear friend, Neysa Borkert, and Angela grew close after meeting in middle school. Both lived in Lehigh Acres which Neysa describes as a lower to middle class neighborhood. Neither had any intention of settling into the life that being from that neighborhood might easily have offered them. Together they joined and were active in almost every club at their school. The two enrolled in middle school drama classes. At times, even though they were great friends, those classes became more like spirited competition between them. Competition served them both as they sought to excel.

Confirming what other childhood friends said, Neysa went on, "Angela never seemed to behave badly or get in serious trouble. It was not as though Angela was not around it for she was. It just seemed that she never sought to get involved with it. There was a strength that Angela had that most others only wish they had. She could learn from the mistakes of others without having to make those same mistakes herself." That skill has been a part of Angela for as long as Neysa has known her.

Neysa, now an attorney practicing in Florida, later provided Angela with some stellar and critical legal advice.

Angela's graduation from Lehigh Senior High School brought the end of childhood. Her high level of academic accomplishment won scholarship offers from several universities. She selected an academic scholarship from the University of Central Florida in Orlando.

Her college years were shared with Neysa and new friends she met there: Pippin Haseman, Bernadette Mahoney and Jennifer Murphy were foremost among them.

Pippin tells of the time Angela drove a friend to the airport. While there she saw a young Asian girl of about five years of age attempting to purchase a soda from a vending machine. "Angela provided the needed coins and the girl got her drink. The girl's parents thanked Angela. In the conversation that followed, Angela discovered that they had not been in the USA before. They were going to Disney World but did not know how to drive or how to get there. Angela volunteered to drive them to their hotel and to other places they might like to see. They invited her to spend some time with them beside the hotel pool during their visit and she did. Their little girl began calling her aunt."

Pippin and Bernadette were her roommates for their sophomore and junior years. Toward the end of college Bernadette and Angela somehow lost track of each other but reconnected in an accidental meeting while walking down a busy street in Manhattan. Both had found work there after graduation, and this chance encounter delighted both of them.

Angela and Jennifer worked as food servers at Bennigan's restaurant in Orlando. They were assigned to serve the customers in one section of the restaurant. Their personalities combined with the quality of their service made that the section of choice for many regular customers. Both girls believed that if you had to work in food service you should make it fun for yourself and for your customers.

Another dear friend from college, Mike Roberts, has fond memories of Angela. They met in a public relations class. He recalls how Angela's infectious laugh often rolled across the classroom.

He found her to be inspirational too. During college he often travelled and worked abroad. Each time he returned to the classroom he had to scramble to catch up with what he had missed. Sensing what he was going through, Angela thoughtfully gave him a copy of Kahlil Gibran's *The Prophet.* He identified that book as "one of the sweetest and most thoughtful gifts ever given to him by anyone." She selected the gifts she so frequently gave to others with real forethought. She wanted her gifts to speak to the personal needs of the person to whom she gave them. Mike's wife, Alana added, "The moment I met her I knew why she was such a wonderful friend during college to the man who became my husband. I adore her."

Later in New York City, through Mike's introduction, Angela met and befriended Mike's step-brothers, Josh and Jeremiah Doyle. Mike wanted them to help her ease into her new life in the big city. He also wanted them to benefit from having her as their friend. Long-running threads of friendship are the fabric from which the cloth of life is best woven. Angela has more than a few of her threads in that cloth.

In college Angela was driven by financial need and a strong desire for new experiences. She sought and held a variety of jobs. One was as a counselor at a girls' summer camp that she had first attended as a camper. It was located near her dad's home in the mountains of western North Carolina. Camp Green Cove was just across a lake from the boys' camp, Mondamin, where her father Charlie was employed during the summers. It was their time together each year and both really looked forward to it.

Angela taught rock climbing, tennis and All Camp Activities or ACA. ACA was designed to get reluctant and home-sick campers out of their cabins and doing something they might actually enjoy. She had shown through high school a special talent for getting her classmates moving and involved. Her selection to this special counseling position was a natural.

One incident illustrates her empathy and compassion. Angela had set up a hiking trip that included some rock climbing. One young camper was climbing when her long hair became tangled in the climbing gear. She could not move up or down the rock face. Angela climbed up to help her. To free the camper, Angela had to cut off a large chunk of the girl's beautiful hair. When they got down, the young camper was quite upset at having lost her hair. Angela took her to town to get the girl's hair cut short enough to even it. Just to show her support, Angela had her hair cut short too.

Along for those summers at Green Cove was her sister Dayna who attended as a camper. Dayna was five years younger than Angela. That age difference meant that when they were at home in Florida they did not often spend quality time together. They were not in the same schools and not in the same activities. Angela was also always working or involved in something at school. The sisters cherished their time of summer fun together. Dayna's death in 2004 meant the camp time they had together with dad Charlie made these months and the memories even more important.

The reflections of Angela's friends were vivid and provided lovingly. Her childhood and college years impacted the lives of many young friends. They adored her and learned about life by watching her handle her own life. She was good for them. Not surprisingly, they all remain her friends to this day.

Angela graduated in 2000 with a bachelor's degree. Her major was in mass communications with a minor in creative writing. Her studies had gone well and she was ready.

Her college degree opened the door to significant employment opportunities. The degree could help her get a good job and start a career. Perhaps as important as her college degree were the values and the character she embodied. When her life took its tragic turn, it was her strength of character that allowed her to recover.

She was born in Alabama and had moved to Florida early in grade school. Until her graduation from college,

Angela had lived almost all of her life in Florida. Now it seemed that the best opportunities would take her away from her home state. In fact, the very best of those opportunities was in New York City. It was time to take on the world. She was ready for New York City.

2

Working in New York City

How does a fresh graduate move from a Florida university to a desirable position in a New York City public relations firm? One of the more fortunate decisions she made while attending UCF was to find a summer internship between her junior and senior year. That internship took her to New York City for a summer of employment with a major marketing and public relations firm. There she met and worked with Donetta Allen. She was a semester ahead of Angela and attended a different university. She and Angela really got along and each respected the work of the other. After their summer internships ended, Donetta returned to her school, quickly graduated and found employment at another firm in Manhattan, Hunter Public Relations. Once there, she told her manager that she knew a top prospect who would be graduating from college in a few months. She urged the company to invite Angela Leigh Tucker in for an interview.

They did. Hunter liked what they saw and heard in the interview and offered Angela employment. She grabbed it. She was not certain what she was getting herself into, but she had never required certainty when making important decisions. She was game for a professional and personal life in a distant city that she knew very little about. Thus began an eight-year career with Hunter.

She needed a place to live. Along came Jackie Gonzalez with a most generous offer. Angela had worked for Jackie in her summer internship. She told Angela that she was about to move from her apartment to another. If Angela was interested she should talk to the landlord. It was a nice two bedroom apartment in Pelham. Angela decided to jump on it. She lived there for several years until she met and married her husband Rich.

How strong and lasting has the relationship bond between these two women remained over the years? I happened to be in the car with Angela one day when her cell phone rang. It was one year after her brain injury. Her friend Jackie was calling with a most significant request: would Angela consider being the Godmother for her new baby, a little girl she named Angelica? Angela asked a couple of questions to be sure that Jackie was certain that she wanted her in that important role. Convinced that she did, Angela smiled and accepted with warm words of appreciation. What a moment that was. This thoughtful request confirmed Angela's value, brain injured or not, in the lives of her friends. It demonstrated the staying power of the friendships Angela formed over the years.

Her new job was going nicely. The same qualities that had made her a leader in high school and college would bring her success at Hunter Public Relations.

Hunter had no way of knowing just how much talent came in her five-foot, four-inch frame. Over the next eight years, Angela accepted and handled everything Hunter asked of her. She invested herself in a variety of assignments. Her performance shined and she became a vice president of the firm at age twenty-nine.

Angela worked hard as did all the professionals at Hunter, but she played hard too. She sometimes grabbed the microphone on Karaoke night at Junno's on Downing Street in the Village. The Hunter gang also favored Winnie's in China Town. She loved sharing her beautiful singing voice with the delighted crowd. Sometimes, to be better seen and heard, she might end up on a table top from which the performance would continue. She believed that life was to be lived to the fullest. Where better to live a full life than in the Big Apple? She did it all.

Her non-work life was not all wine and cheese. She was a giver and not a taker. Angela sought and took on a difficult volunteer position. She became a mentor for an eighth grade girl, Melissa Barba, whose family was from Ecuador. She found the girl through a program established by St. Jude school in the Inwood neighborhood. Melissa needed the positive influence of a successful role model. Angela needed a little sister. Theirs was a mutually beneficial relationship. Melissa later became an accomplished student at Penn State University where she studied International Politics and National Security and was selected as the MVP of her college tennis team. Melissa and Angela continue to value this relationship that could logically have run its course by now, but with Angela – once a friend, always a friend.

Angela was interested in dating and she did. But she was selective. Even in New York City, her type of man was not easy to find. Many of the men she met were of little interest to her. She was not about to invest even one date with them. With her steady work-related travel and other demands for her time, she did not need another project. Dating was not her top priority.

However, Angela's priorities began to change when she met Rich Betancourt, who was employed as a sales person at the Guitar Center. Later, advancing his career, he worked at Best Music Rental Services in Long Island City as the sales and office manager. His friend and subordinate there, Ricardo Wilkinson, describes Rich as a perfectionist who insisted on perfection in others. Ricardo says that Rich was a persistent yet motivating boss. He and others at Best benefitted from having Rich Betancourt in their midst.

Like Angela, Rich had a reputation for being selective. He had been married once before. Since his divorce he had carried with him the disappointment and emotional scars that had proven tough to heal. Rich was a sensitive person, perhaps more wounded by divorce than most of the general population. He seemed to be in no real hurry to make another commitment. He had his job and his music to see him through. Yet when he met Angela, those around him knew he had fallen hard for her. They began dating. He talked about her with his friends. He sent her flowers frequently and began writing songs for and about her. The fellow was, as they say, smitten. She was too!

Music was more than Rich's vocation. It was also his passion. He formed and led a five-piece band called the "Cellar Poets." They played local gigs and recorded an album. Rich wrote much of what they played and handled some of the vocals. He played guitar and keyboard. The group had been scheduled to play just days after his tragic death. Best Music sales manager and band member, Damon Jackson, said that the "show" went on as scheduled that night, but the band remained silent on the stage and has been unwilling and unable to perform since. Their memories of him are much too fresh even two years after his death.

Having secured a strong commitment from each other, neither Rich nor Angela felt the need to marry quickly. After dating for four years, they married on September 22, 2007 in a simple outdoor chapel in the woods at Camp Ton-A-Wandah in Flat Rock, North Carolina. Angela was twenty-nine and Rich was thirty-seven. Family and a few friends were there to share their joy. Those who attended felt the love flowing between these exceptional young people.

Soon after they were married, they thought it time to buy a home out of the city. They sought a home in a small town somewhere not too far from a commuter train line. They liked the feel of the communities that ran up the Hudson River from Manhattan, even though they would have a long commuter train ride to get to work.

A happy couple

Their work schedules were demanding and always changing. The likelihood was high that they would often pass like ships in the night. But having a home of their own away from the city was really important. They wanted hobby space and a garden. They wanted a patio to use for cook-outs. They even wanted to have grass to cut.

They also had a dog. Actually Angela brought a dog to the marriage. Her dog Moses needed a place to play and that was just one more reason to find and buy a home away from the city.

Moses enjoys his new home

Moses, a Yorkshire terrier, was the orphaned pet of Angela's sister Dayna, who died three years earlier in a single-car crash. She was only twenty-one years old.

Angela could not bring herself to get rid of her sister's dog. Even though a dog was the last thing she really needed in her busy life, she adopted him.

He lived like a crown prince. Moses had some serious health problems. Those problems meant Angela spent hundreds of dollars with veterinarians. In a loving tribute to her sister, Angela never counted the dollars she was spending.

The search for a home was on. When the young couple found the home of their dreams they knew it. Just six months after their marriage, they were moving in. The home was in the Floridan Estates neighborhood close to the little village of Putnam Valley. The neighborhood, originally a summer and weekend retreat for city dwellers, consisted of dozens of summer cottages, a couple of small fishing lakes, an active stream, a huge community pool, picnic area and some heavily wooded walking trails. Over the years, most of the cottages had been winterized and converted to year-round living. A few of the neighbors were commuters; others were retired or worked close to Putnam Valley. It was a nice mix of people and they watched out for each other.

The young Betancourts purchased one of three homes that had been originally built for year-round living. It was a little larger than many in the neighborhood and had a full apartment on the second floor with a private entrance. Angela planned to invite her mother to move from Florida to live in that apartment. Upon moving in they began to paint and decorate.

They finished the dining room first and soon started with the painting and window treatment for the other rooms.

Happy home in Floridan

They made certain that the home was nicely furnished, not fancy but certainly comfortable. Rich brought his family heirloom grand piano to play. He set up a recording studio in a small upstairs room. Within weeks of their move, the home was warm and welcoming.

They trimmed the outside bushes, cleaned the deck and the traditional wood burning grill. They wasted no time getting ready for a summer of outdoor fun. On July 4th weekend they had friends over for a grand cook-out. Entertaining was something they were good at and enjoyed doing.

Life had been good before the move and became even better since. They talked of having babies to fill the available space in the home and in their abundant hearts.

Angela Leigh Tucker as told by Bill Ramsey

3

Changing Everything with the Crash

On Thursday July 31, 2008, Rich and Angela arose early as they usually did. They drove into the city together because they planned to end the day at the Yankees baseball game.

The week or two leading up to this day had been an especially busy time for Angela. As a VP at Hunter Public Relations she had been assigned a major client: a California wine producer. The upcoming trade show, organized by *Outdoor Retailer*, was a significant and important event for her client. It was scheduled to begin the following week at Salt Palace Convention Center in Salt Lake City, Utah. Angela was responsible for much more than just showing up, drinking the client's wine and having a good time. That would have been easy for her. She was an old hand at the work-hard, party-hard world of public relations.

She did, for her clients, many of the tasks a fulltime event and business meeting planner would do. She facilitated and led pre-event brain-storming sessions.

Then when the event was rolling along, clients were free to connect with and focus their complete attention upon their customers. Under Angela's watchful eye, her Hunter team intended to make this event work so smoothly that no one would be aware of the detailed planning and execution that had gone into it. She had done events like this before. They had gone well and that is part of the reason why she had earned her promotion.

For every one of these critical client events, Angela put in extraordinarily long hours. Many nights in the previous weeks, Rich had driven to the commuter train station to meet one of the last trains out of the city. A 10 PM arrival had become the norm.

The management at Hunter appreciated the effort she was making, but they did not intend to allow her job to wreck her new marriage. They were also concerned that Angela could be worn out before the client event ever started. She was to fly out in a couple of days, and once there the demands placed on her would be considerable. She needed to be fresh and rested upon arrival.

As the busy day played out in the office, Angela argued that she should keep working that evening and skip the baseball game. She did have that major client event the following week. Her manager and co-workers argued just as vigorously that she needed a night off. She relented and Rich picked her up for the short drive to the ball park.

A New York Yankees baseball game was a pleasant way for Angela and Rich to spend a mid-summer evening. The old Yankee Stadium was in its last season giving this last trip to that stately old ballpark special significance. The Yankees would play the following season in an all-new stadium. The weather was typical for a late July night in the city; hot and humid but tolerable. For Rich and Angela, being together was all that really mattered.

The ballpark food was enjoyable. The crowd of over 53,000 was as much fun to watch as the game. The Yankee opponents that night were the Los Angeles Angels (Imagine, Angela at an Angels game.) The final score, Angels 12—Yankees 6, was not what Yankee fans had wanted. The Yankees had won eight in a row since the All-Star break, and their fans had wanted to see the winning streak extended. The young couple didn't care much one way or the other. This night was about being together.

Before leaving their seats Angela called her dad in North Carolina to tell him where they were and what a wonderful evening they had had together. She had a habit of calling him. She frequently called her mother in Florida too. The call to her dad that evening had to have been reassuring to him. Fathers are always interested in hearing their married daughters indicate marital joy.

Angela ended that call to her father as she always did when calling him: "I love you, Daddy."

They headed for the parking lot to start the drive home. It would be a short night followed by another long day at their offices. Their route would take them up the Deegan Expressway and then on to Putnam Valley.

As was their custom, they undoubtedly listened to some music on the way home. They both loved to listen to music and sing along together – such fine voices, such harmony.

Rich was something of a frustrated musician. He had recorded some of the original songs he had written for Angela and put them on a personal CD for her to enjoy. His soft vocals were backed by his own acoustic guitar work. Those songs were one way that Rich expressed his love for his wonderful wife. Angela cannot recall what they were listening to that evening, but a safe guess would have some of his love tunes in the mix. Carefree and in love is the best way to end any day.

At this late hour the ride home would not take as long as usual, perhaps just over an hour from the

34

ballpark to their driveway. They were on the Major Deegan Expressway and less than an hour from home when a fast-moving tractor-trailer literally hurtled across the high concrete median barrier and crushed their SUV.

The crash scene showed absolute devastation; one damaged tractor-trailer, its driver walking around surveying the scene, one crushed personal vehicle containing two passengers, and sirens and flashing lights from a gathering of police and first responder vehicles. The air was filled with the mixed odors always present near a major crash; raw fuel, rubber, and exhaust fumes blend with those of the medications being administered to the survivor. The crash was head-on and the impact incredibly violent. The make and model of Rich's SUV were not easy to identify.

Instantaneous and horrific, the crash was captured by one of the video cameras positioned along the highway. Angela has not watched the video recording and has no plans to do so. No purpose would be served by her watching something so horrid.

It is appropriate to call this a crash because to call it an accident implies a kind of fault-free randomness that is not the usual cause of most highway wrecks. This crash was not an accident. This truck was speeding, operated recklessly by a driver who had left on his route late that day.

How fast is a blink of an eye? That is how long the crash took. There was no long spinning slide with a couple of seconds to scream or look toward your partner. The words "never knew what hit them" describe it well.

4

Surviving the First Hour

The crash scene changed from one of a speeding truck leaping across the highway median to one of a speedy emergency response.

Rich was obviously dead. This was not the time to say that he had "passed away" or he was "gone." To soften the words would not change the devastating truth.

Angela was unconscious and pinned in the crushed vehicle. She had been bounced and twisted as the SUV folded in around her. Both she and Rich had seat belts on as they always did. Seat belts and deployed airbags had made little difference. The impact was just too great.

The emergency responders who arrived first had a choice to make. They would have liked to take their time in determining her condition and carefully extract her without causing more damage. It was immediately obvious that Angela had little time left. They had to move deliberately but they knew she had to be transported to a trauma center at once. They did not have the luxury of an extra ten minutes to get her out. Her respiration was so faint as to be easily missed. They applied an Ambu-bag and mask to assist her in breathing. She would need a tracheal intubation upon arrival at the trauma center.

Based upon their experience with violent crashes, rescue teams were almost certain that Angela had suffered severe injuries to her brain and neck. She was later found to have suffered a significant break to her Atlas/Axis. The Atlas (C1) is the first vertebra and is responsible for supporting the head. It had been fractured. Just below it is the Axis. Together they connect the skull and the spine. A break in the Atlas is of major concern because the brain stem passes through it and extends down to the Axis. Moving her without the use of proper procedures and neck support could have paralyzed her or ended her life right then and there. After properly immobilizing her neck, they skillfully removed her from the crushed vehicle and secured her to the board she would be transported upon. (See the book cover photo of the scene.)

She had multiple broken bones but the gift of being deeply unconscious spared her the excruciating pain of being extracted and transported. The EMS team had their hands quite full.

The EMS team determined that travel time to the hospital by ambulance might be more time than Angela had left. It was also obvious that she needed the talents of a nurse and a paramedic ASAP. Those talents could arrive in a timely way only if a helicopter could get there and land in time. A medical evacuation helicopter based at Westchester Medical Center was called.

The helicopter was guided to the scene, in part, by the miles of tail lights on the highway below. At the end of those lights were the flashing lights of all the emergency equipment vehicles: fire trucks, police cars and ambulances were there from two jurisdictions. The crash occurred on the line between the city of New York and that of Yonkers.

The pilot that night, Bill Palmer, had flown a helicopter during the Vietnam war. He circled the crash site once from high above to see if there was a safe landing possibility. He circled a second time at a lower altitude, standard procedure, to look more closely at the crash. The flight crew listened to the communications from the EMT's on the ground about whether they thought the crash victim had a chance of surviving. There was no sense in attempting a landing in the dark if the victim showed no signs of making it or had already expired.

Pilot Palmer had a way of reducing the tension for himself and other life flight crew members. On this night he joked as he piloted the helicopter onto a landing area much less than ideal. He had to set the copter down onto the highway between two high concrete retaining walls that caused the wash of the wind from the copter's blades to be unusually turbulent. There were concrete lane dividers and highway light stanchions in the landing area. Palmer commented that he was not sure who was landing that copter but he didn't believe he was alone in doing it.

A nurse, Jenna Canavan, and two experienced paramedics, Rob Kallen and Ken Reardon, stepped out of the helicopter less than twenty minutes after receiving the call. Those EMS responders already had Angela secured to the body board and they were carrying her toward the copter. She was loaded aboard and the pilot lifted off for an eight-minute flight to the trauma center at Westchester Medical Center. The pilot's bold decision and professional skill in landing that night helped save Angela's life.

Had the helicopter pilot decided the landing site was too risky or had wind and weather been bad, he could not have attempted the landing. Angela's initial care and transport would have been left to EMS personnel. They do a great job but an ambulance is not as well equipped as a life flight helicopter and would have taken more time to transport her. Life flight nurses and paramedics also have had much more training and experience than EMS teams in dealing with severe trauma.

Had she been transported by ambulance, Angela would have been taken to a nearby hospital emergency room with much less experience in dealing with severe trauma. In an ordinary ER, her survival would have been a mixture of luck and ER medicine. Even if she had survived, permanent and severe damage could have made it impossible for her to recover enough to live an independent life. Some may call the whole sequence of events plain old luck. Those that believe in God would challenge the notion that luck was what saved her. To many it seemed that God had smiled upon her. The angels had won again, but this time it was not the baseball Angels.

During the flight the crew conducted itself like an intensive care unit or ICU in the sky. While communicating with Westchester about their inbound patient they began procedures they were qualified to perform. Westchester Medical Center has a long history of success in effectively dealing with severe trauma.

The first hour after a traumatic injury is critical to survival and recovery. It is often referred to as the "Golden Hour of Medicine." The effort to get Angela to the trauma center had saved some of that first hour for the trauma team awaiting her there.

If the first hours after the crash were critical, the next day was only slightly less so. Vital signs were monitored in the ICU. The full extent of her injuries was daunting: left frontal hemorrhage, right parietal contusion, bilateral sub-arachnoid hemorrhage, bi-frontal hemorrhagic contusions, intra-ventricular hemorrhage, left occipital condoyle (skull) fracture, fracture of the C1 vertebrae, left scapulae (shoulder blade) fracture, left rib fractures of 1, 2, and 3, and a third nerve palsy. When that third cranial nerve is damaged, the muscles that control the movement of the eyeball do not operate properly. Her mouth and teeth had also been significantly damaged.

Angela scored a 3 on the Glasgow coma scale. That scale has a range of scores from a low of 3 to top score of 15. The 3 meant that in eye-opening, verbal or motor measurement, she had NO RESPONSE. To state it bluntly, her brain and bones were so severely injured that her survival prospects did not look at all good.

Surgical procedures and their sequencing kept her medical team busy. With so much to do just where should they begin? Of course, dealing with the brain trauma had to come before taking care of her broken bones. It was critical to stop any bleeding in the brain. Fluid build-up and pressure from swelling of the brain needed to be relieved.

There was plenty of praying, monitoring and waiting as the trauma team performed the necessary procedures. Hospital personnel are not without a spiritual side.

Outside the ICU another drama was being played out. The crash scene had been chaotic. The late hour and darkness made things more difficult for the responders. What remained of the Ford Explorer was hauled away from the crash scene. Witnesses later described it as looking like a metal pancake.

It may be hard to imagine but the identity of the crash victims was not initially known to the hospital. The hospital did not know who to contact. Well into the late afternoon of the next day, no one outside the hospital had heard anything. Was anyone in charge of getting the families found and notified?

Angela's cell phone fell out of their SUV along the route used to tow it to the scrap yard. The phone was not returned until days later when some good Samaritan called the "in case of emergency number" stored in the phone. That call, intended to return the missing cell phone, was not a part of the victim identity process. Had the cell phone been immediately recovered at the crash scene, it would have been helpful in the identification of Rich and Angela and in the notification of their parents.

It was not at all like Angela or Rich to ever miss work. They were dedicated and loved their jobs. If they did have to miss work they always called. Their co-workers at Best Music and at Hunter Public Relations knew that about both of them. Where were they? What was up?

After lunch on Friday afternoon, Angela's friend and co-worker, Christine Reardon, could no longer stand not knowing why she had not come in or called. Christine went on-line to survey local newspaper accounts of over-night accidents. She found an article posted in one paper that briefly reported on a severe crash had occurred along the Major Deegan. She knew that was the route that Rich and Angela were likely to have used to drive home after the game. The article was short and contained scant accident details and no victim names. It did say the crash had been devastating: a Ford Explorer had been hit head-on in a cross-over crash involving a

44

semi-truck, that a young man had been declared dead at the scene, and that a young woman had been flown out by evacuation helicopter. It did not name the victims or the destination hospital.

Christine was immediately concerned. Could the article be describing Rich and Angela? She sought to pin down the identification of the victims. Having grown up in Westchester, she was familiar with the local hospitals. She first called Bronxville Hospital and was told they had no admissions that matched her description.

Her second call was to Westchester Medical Center. They said that two crash victims were brought near midnight. When Christine offered the names of Angela and Rich, the hospital would not disclose anything to her. She was not a family member. The federal Health Information Patient Privacy Act (HIPPA), intended to protect patient privacy, meant the hospital could not and would not provide any patient information to a non-family member. However, they did admit that the descriptions she provided of Rich and Angela seemed to match the descriptions of two people who had been brought in. The hospital stated that no information about family contacts was found on the crash victims. They wanted to contact the families but had no way to start the process. Law enforcement did not yet have any information either.

Now, very alarmed by her discovery, Christine sought advice as to how to proceed from Jon Lyon, Angela's longtime boss and friend. They contacted the hospital again and provided the name and phone number of Angela's mother in Florida. Hunter called Perry Winston, the company president and CEO at Best Music. The folks at Hunter wanted to know if the folks at Best had any information. Was Rich at work and could he help them find Angela? Best Music had not seen him that day and had been wondering where he was and why he had not called in.

The employees at both companies now had real reason to worry. Hunter asked Best Music to contact his parents or his sister Denise in nearby Tenafly, New Jersey. Best Music had their number, Hunter did not. Through this uneven process the hospital finally had the information it needed to contact the families. The notification process had taken more than sixteen hours after the crash.

Still not sure what they would find once they got to Westchester Medical Center, Jon Lyon and Angela's friend and co-worker, Gigi Russo, headed there. Others from the Hunter office had wanted to go but agreed that this was not the time to send a crowd to the hospital.

Rich's family got there quickly from their Tenafly home. They feared they would find a badly injured Rich and Angela. What they were told was so much worse. Gigi, already at the hospital, was the first to meet the Betancourts upon their arrival. She had already made the grim discovery about Rich's death. Not knowing that his family had not yet been told, upon greeting his sister Denise, Gigi expressed her sorrow for their loss. Denise did not know what she meant. The family next spoke with a person from the hospital staff who officially broke the tragic news to them. Their only son and Denise's only sibling had not survived the crash and Angela was hanging onto life by a thin thread. Devastated by the news, somehow they were able to gather themselves and immediately go to Angela's side.

Angela's mother Carol arrived at the hospital as quickly as she could fly in from Florida. Perhaps because of the relationship complications caused by their divorce years before, Angela's father Charlie was not notified until four days after the crash. The first evidence of some family dysfunction had appeared.

Meanwhile, at Hunter, all Angela's friends attempted to console each other. Gigi called the office from the hospital to report that Angela had apparently suffered a severe brain trauma and additional massive injuries. At that moment, Christine could find nothing better or more comforting to do than to search the internet for traumatic brain injury educational items. She had never been close to someone who has had a TBI, and she had much to learn. She discovered that there could be healing; it would take time but it was possible. She joined the others in the office in believing, or at least wanting to believe, that if anyone could recover the use of her brain it was their friend Angela.

Jon Lyon spent that Friday afternoon attempting to calm the employees. He kept them from rushing off to the hospital. It was not easy for him as he was more than a boss to Angela. Handling the situation in the office had fallen on Jon's shoulders because Hunter partners, Jason Winocour and Grace Leong, were both out of town on vacation the day the tragic news had hit the office. Jason was in Paris and Grace was at the beach. Tearfully, Jon called them and both made plans to return immediately to the office.

No one wanted to go home after work that Friday and be alone with their concerns. Several actually stayed together for the weekend. The emotional waves of this trauma rolled far beyond the confines of the hospital and washed over many people.

5

Moving Beyond Coma and Surgery

Angela will survive. That much is known after week one. However, that is about the limit of what was known with certainty. Only time would tell how much actual recovery there would be and how many years that recovery would take. Yes, years!

Many survivors of brain injuries come to consider the day of their injury to be the day of their second birth. In the months to come, Angela came to view it that way too.

This second birth is not like any infant birth. A newborn baby is learning everything for the first time. New brains and skulls are growing larger as the learning is taking place. Traumatic brain injuries are different. Unlike a new baby, brain injured adults are not starting with a fresh, un-programmed and growing brain. The more mature brains of older children and adults are not learning for the first time. They are re-learning what they once knew: the big things like how to walk or speak

49

again and simple tasks like how to brush their teeth, take a shower and get dressed. The list is daunting.

Re-learning is difficult but it can and does happen. It requires an immense and dedicated effort by the brain injured person with the help of doctors and therapists. Professional help and brain healing time are needed.

Perhaps a helpful analogy would be to compare brain injury recovery in adults to the methods used to recover the lost memory of a computer after a hard-drive crash. Most of what was on the hard-drive before the crash is likely still there, but it has to be recovered and restored. However, portions of its memory may be permanently lost and efforts to recover that lost data may not be successful. So it is with a TBI. The injured brain must be reprogrammed, and sometimes the reprogramming cannot restore everything.

TBI survivors and their support team have no way in the early days of knowing how their brain injuries have affected them. Each survivor's situation is unique. Some brain function may never return. Even years after an injury, some never regain their lost sense of smell and taste, for example. Some have vision problems. Personality changes occur; some are more mellow while others are more edgy than they were before their injury. Many have short-term memory and cognition issues to manage. It would take weeks to discover how Angela's injury was going to manifest itself. It was a long wait for those who knew and loved her.

There is no completely standard protocol for treating brain injuries. All those in recovery are not on exactly the same recovery program or schedule. That is refreshing and hopeful. It illustrates that these people were unique before their injuries and that they are still unique after the injuries. Retaining one's individuality and uniqueness is a positive thing even when it comes with the added challenge of recovering from a brain injury.

With her life temporarily on hold while in her coma, those around Angela continued to deal with the aftermath of the crash. For example, in keeping with the traditions of his father's religious beliefs, Rich's funeral was conducted on Sunday within forty-eight hours after the crash. Seven weeks after the funeral, on September 22, the first anniversary of the young couple's 2007 wedding passed quietly.

The reality was that for everyone but Angela, life was moving on. Of course, all who knew and loved her wanted to know when and in what condition Angela might rejoin them. It would be several weeks before they had any real indication.

Most of us tend to think of coma as being equivalent to sleep. We have all seen movies and television shows where a comatose person suddenly wakes up and begins dialogue with those at their side. It doesn't happen that way.

A coma is not like a good night of sleep. Sleep involves changing patterns and dreaming. Brain wave analysis shows coma to be very different.

Therapy cannot begin during the time in a coma. However, other medical procedures and surgeries are performed as needed. During a coma the injured brain is on its own to begin the long and uncertain healing process.

As the weeks passed at Westchester, Angela remained in a coma. She was unaware of the people serving her; she will never know who they were or how they helped.

Since her youth, she had demonstrated leadership qualities and inspired those around her. But this was a different challenge for her. How could she possibly lead now? She was in a deep coma.

Perhaps those treating her and those praying for her recovery were moved by her youth? Perhaps they were drawn in by a growing awareness of how completely devastating the crash had been, the losses she had suffered, and by doubts about her recovering to live anything resembling a "normal" life. Whatever she needed to lead them she projected from deep within her coma; they seemed to be following her unspoken inspiration.

Within hours and for days after the crash, people she had known all her life were dropping everything and planning to fly or drive in for a visit to the hospital. Those who felt the need to be there included grade school friends from Florida, co-workers at Hunter PR, clients from around the country, new neighbors from her Floridan community and, of course, her family. They wanted to be near her. They all wanted to do what they could. Something. Anything.

One example illustrates the extent of her friend's love and desire to help. Her co-worker Gigi Russo and boss Jon Lyon knew that Angela and Rich had two new cats and her dog Moses. They realized those pets needed care so they drove to Putnam Valley to check on them. They arrived there about five on Saturday morning. They had some difficulty finding the house in the dark. They had been given a ring of Angela's keys upon leaving the hospital. One of those keys would surely open the door. One did.

The cats and the dog were fine. The cats were adopted and relocated to the home of co-worker, Samara Mormar. Moses, the dog, was to stay with Melissa Curcio until Angela was once again able to care for him.

Having performed their task, they headed back to the city. Part way there, Gigi remembered having seen a mango on the counter in the kitchen. Knowing the mango was going to ripen, rot and smell, she insisted on turning back to retrieve that mango. They did. I first thought of this story as odd and even a little funny. Then I saw what it really represented. Tied-up in emotional knots and not seeing any better way to help their friend, they did the only thing they knew they could do at that moment. They saved her mango.

From the collection of people streaming into the hospital to visit Angela, most meeting each other for the first time, an informal team began to form. When they found a way to help they did so without being asked or expecting pay-back. For example, in an attempt to keep her connected they would read about current events from the newspaper. Their help took many forms and continued to play out over the weeks and months of her recovery.

One of the first to come and one of the most interesting and important was Mair Culbreth. Angela's dad Charlie had remarried a woman named Mary Wall. Mair was Mary Wall's daughter and Angela's step-sister. She lived and worked in San Francisco. As a result, the two young women had never spent much time together. Mair had been a bridesmaid in Angela's wedding. In their limited time together a bond formed. She knew, without Angela being able to tell her, that she was needed at her side. She left her job and her home and spent weeks at Angela's bedside. When the New York phase of Angela's recovery concluded, Mair stayed involved and relocated with her to the mountains of western North Carolina where Charlie and Mary Wall lived.

Mair is a bright and clear thinking person. Perhaps more than anyone else, she managed the scene and stayed calm as others fell apart or acted in emotional ways that did not always seem to benefit Angela.

During Angela's coma and into the early weeks of her recovery, Mair collected information concerning the traumatic brain injury recovery program that Angela would follow. She got to know the people involved. Like Angela, Mair had lived and worked in a major city. She thought it likely that she could make accurate projections about what Angela would want to have happen when key decisions needed to be made. She confirmed much of what she believed about Angela by having significant conversations with Angela's friends and co-workers when they visited. She was not winging it or guessing; rather she was making informed choices. She vowed to be Angela's advocate until she had recovered sufficiently that she could do it for herself. That was not going to be anytime soon.

It was necessary for someone to direct the endless flood of visitor traffic. Mair did that too. Everyone came with the intention of helping. Often they unintentionally presented challenges and complications. Sometimes there were just too many visitors there all at once. Some came to offer sympathy. Even early in her recovery and fresh off her coma, Angela didn't really desire sympathy. Others came to pump her up and issue a charge to get well soon. The next visitor might attempt to reassure and comfort her. All were well-intentioned and searching for a way to help but at times the right words can be impossible for visitors to find. They did the best they could but the busy hospital room was confusing for Angela and often conflicted with her daily schedule and needs.

Mair tried to monitor everything that was going on. She kept track of the complicated medical and therapy schedule. She recorded the flowers and gifts that arrived daily.

Mair knew how many people were interested in following Angela's progress so she created an account for her on www.CaringBridge.org and posted daily updates there. In the months following the crash, over 43,000 people would follow those updates. When Angela was finally strong enough to do it, she posted her own updates. Obviously, Angela was touching lives of those who had never met her and never would.

Mair also acted as mediator when disagreements arose between the family and the medical/ therapy team. Angela's mother played a critically important role, but she often failed to step away from the bedside to get some rest. At times, she was unable to successfully step back emotionally. Mair provided stability.

Financially, Mair could not afford to be in New York for the weeks that she intended to stay. She made a real sacrifice when she could have taken an easier way out, but Angela desperately needed her help.

When I asked Mair months later about what she had done and why she had done it, she was completely forthcoming in her answers. At that time she was about to move out of the Tucker home in North Carolina and return to her personal life. Mair looked back and recalled several very happy moments over the months that she had been near Angela. There was the first weekend in the rehab hospital when Angela sang "Ain't no sunshine when she's gone." Although Angela's voice was as weak and broken as she was, the desire to sing was returning to her life. Also in the succession of happy times was the unassisted shower Angela took on January 1st when she had regained enough balance to safely stand in the shower. Moments like these, in the life of a recovering TBI survivor, are about as big as it gets on the way back.

She had also been with Angela through some difficult moments. She was there when, in October 2008, weeks after the July 31st crash, a person came from the New York state court system to discuss guardianship issues. Angela's parents could not agree on becoming joint guardians. Mom Carol insisted on being the controlling guardian. Dad Charlie saw that she was making progress and thought the need for a guardian was not yet clear and that the decision should be postponed. Mair defended Angela's freedom of choice and forestalled Carol's efforts to take over.

The guardianship turmoil was stressful for Angela as she had always attempted to please people, especially her mother. When disagreements occurred at her bedside while she was still comatose, a measureable change in her heart rate and blood pressure resulted. How can a person in a coma sense the dysfunction occurring near her and register a reaction to it? We don't know, but clearly the patient needs a quiet and reassuring environment that allows the brain to heal. Mair's parents had divorced years earlier so she anticipated dealing with the strained nature of the relationship between Angela's parents.

Angela's parents, Carol and Charlie had been divorced for many years. It had to be difficult for both of them to be thrust into this situation. They had lost their only other child, Dayna, several years earlier and neither could even imagine now losing Angela. Had Angela's sister Dayna lived, she likely would have filled the role that Mair did. Mair knew how important a sister can be as her own sister is a vital part of her life.

Carol and Charlie found themselves once again under the same roof, living in Angela's house in order to save money and to be close to the hospital where she was recovering. Angela was not the only person suffering.

There is a very good reason for mentioning this family's dysfunction. My intention is not to embarrass anyone or to choose sides. The reason for describing the dysfunction is simple. All families who have a loved one with an unexpected brain injury (and these injuries are never expected) face new challenges. Brain injuries are real game-changers for those who suffer them and, unavoidably, for the family.

Even a family with little history of dysfunction is apt to encounter new stress-causing moments. It is best to anticipate them, accept them as inevitable and deal with them when they occur. Often that dealing can require professional help which the therapy team and social workers at the rehabilitation hospital are well equipped to provide.

One of the common disagreements between family members concerns knowing how hard to allow therapists to push their loved one in therapy sessions. It is easy for parents to become overly protective of their injured adult "child." The same can be said of a spouse or the siblings of the injured. Some over-protecting was going on here.

I asked Mair to summarize her several months' experience with Angela. She contended that she got more from Angela than she ever gave. From her, Mair obtained a deeper appreciation for life.

Even before the crash Mair claimed to have learned a lot from Angela. For example, she knew Angela had always had a well-conceived and consistent plan for her life. Mair also had a plan but she felt it was less focused and more fluid. Mair had an undergraduate degree in multi-disciplinary studies with a minor nuclear engineering. She had followed that up with a Master's degree in Kinesiology. Next she was to embark on the pursuit of a PhD in dance studies. At its core, her studies were all about medicine and the movement of the human body. She had a plan but it evolved as she went along. Mair's collective skills left her well equipped to help Angela.

Angela had established a career and life plan while in undergraduate school and had not wavered from it. She had been on a fast track to achieving that plan. Mair believed that at the age of thirty "Angela had it all and lost it all." Yet Angela never seemed to see the loss that way. Although she would never have wanted to have her life include such massive tragedy, Angela persisted in seeing her survival as a gift that presented her with a chance to start over. Her plans changed with the crash but with the initiation of therapy she became fully engaged in planning her new life.

Could Angela have survived through this most challenging time without Mair's doing as much as she did? The answer is likely yes; she could have. Did Angela do much better with Mair's help than she would have done without her help? Of course she did.

After almost four weeks, Angela was still healing at Westchester Medical Center where numerous surgical procedures were completed. Westchester does not provide therapy for those with brain injuries so she would soon leave for a facility that did. Angela was in a coma but showing signs of emerging from it. However, therapy could not start until she was conscious and alert enough to participate in it.

On August 27th, just 27days since the crash, she was still comatose, but Westchester had done all it could for her. She would awake in a few days at Helen Hayes Hospital. The hard work of therapy for the brain injury was about to begin.

Angela has no recollection of anything or anyone from those Westchester weeks. She sincerely wishes that she had known their names so she could personally thank them. They did a great job.

Angela finally awakened at Helen Hayes and slowly discovered what had occurred. She found herself in a hospital bed. She was carefully told that she was in a car crash. To this day she has no memory of what happened; it had happened so quickly and with such a violent impact.

She was told of her C1 vertebra break. A halo type device surgically applied by the Westchester team secured her head and neck. It is unusual for a brain injured person to be discharged and moved to a rehabilitation hospital while still requiring a halo. She was. There was obvious risk involved with beginning the therapy in her condition but begin it must. She needed to get moving to get better.

Angela was not initially told that her husband Rich died in the crash. Bad news must be given in small doses. She was told days later. Actually, the news of his death had to be given to her at least three different times. The last time, when told by dad Charlie, Angela finally understood. She had no tears because she had yet to regain any sense of emotional sadness about anything that had happened. Brain injuries can block the return of expected emotions.

Everyone was happy that Angela was out of the coma. At the same time, everyone was sad that she had so much bad news left to hear and adjust to. No one denied the harsh realities, least of all Angela herself.

If her coma was a blessing, it was because the physical and emotional pain that she would otherwise suffer was delayed for a time. There are medical advantages to a coma in cases of severe injuries. Surgical procedures can take place with the patient unaware of them. The broken body and damaged brain start to heal. Although it may be difficult to accept this point of view, a patient's time in a coma has some positive aspects.

Beyond all the medical and emotional issues, the family had to face the significant issue of finances. The injured person is not the only person who soon runs into financial complications. Being there to help the patient is expensive and third party expenses are not included as a part of any insurance coverage. Who chips in and just how much do they contribute to extraordinary expenses like temporary housing and groceries?

These problems are worse if the patient is recovering in a city far from family as Angela was. The patient may be in a rehabilitation facility for an extended stay. Who visits and when do they visit while the patient is in the hospital? How long can they stay? Who travels back home to return to work? Can a fair schedule for sharing the care burden be developed? Where does the extra money come from? The questions are many and difficult.

The many complications experienced during recovery soon ripple out to involve more people and more issues. Therapy moves ahead but the rate of recovery cannot be rushed. Family and close friends love the patient and wish for a speedy return to independent living. However, after a few weeks they may find themselves asking, "Does this injury really have to disrupt my life too?" Unfortunately, it usually does.

Angela Leigh Tucker as told by Bill Ramsey

6

Moving on to Rehabilitation

With Angela's broken bones beginning to heal, it was time to turn full attention to her injured brain. That is what rehab facilities do. Helen Hayes Hospital does it particularly well and has for many years. The hospital is named for benefactor Helen Hayes (1900 -1993) who was known as the queen of the Broadway stage. Less well recognized was her philanthropic work. She took a special interest in the rehabilitation programs offered at the hospital that came to bear her name.

This non-profit rehab hospital is situated on a hill overlooking the Hudson River several miles north of Manhattan in West Haverstraw, NY. Angela's fourth floor room had a commanding view of the gardens and the river below. However, Angela was not able to get over to the window to enjoy it.

The hospital staff stood ready to do for Angela what they have done for thousands of brain injured people over the years. From the day of her admission, they knew they had just a few weeks, perhaps eight, to work with her before her insurance would no longer cover their therapy. Insurance policies provide only that long even though the actual healing often takes much longer. Eight weeks is very little time for one so badly injured. This tight time limit meant Angela had to do the therapy sessions even when she felt too physically weak or emotionally drained to do them. She mustered the strength and courage to keep herself and her therapists on task.

Assessment of each new patient begins upon arrival and continues on a regular basis until the patient is discharged. Angela's broken bones and six weeks in a coma had to be factored into that assessment as they planned for initial therapy. The movement required in physical therapy would start with muscles made weak from weeks of disuse and broken bones critical to supporting her body just beginning to knit. If brain-injured patients have suffered no broken bones, no surgery and no coma, they are better able to meet the physical demands of therapy and the tight time schedule for its completion before discharge.

As badly injured as her brain had been, Angela had some things going for her. Younger patients with no history of a prior brain injury, psychiatric problems or substance abuse do better in therapy. She had those statistics working for her.

In assessing the brain damage Angela had suffered, doctors hoped to discover as much as possible about what her head had hit during the crash. It would help them in therapy if they could discover the translation, rotation and angular acceleration forces. They wanted to know just what the brain was doing inside the skull at the moment of impact. Was the damage caused by one straight ahead blow or did the skull suffer impact from two or more directions? Did the crash cause her brain to spin a little inside her skull? Sometimes crash scene evidence can provide clues. Unfortunately, in Angela's case, the crash had completely destroyed the vehicle and erased all the useful evidence.

Helen Hayes provides therapy to patients with all types of brain insult or injury. That certainly includes stroke patients. Perhaps this is a good place to clarify how strokes differ from TBI injuries. With one type of stroke there is bleeding into some part of the brain. Bleeding may start when an aneurysm or arterial bulge ruptures and the artery bleeds into the brain.

A second and much more common type of stroke is called an ischemic stroke where blood flow is cut off from a portion of the brain. Usually the ischemic stroke is caused by a blot clot that blocks blood flow to a portion of the brain, resulting in oxygen deprivation and the death of brain cells. Obviously both types can be fatal but should one survive either of these, an MRI can often show just where the stroke caused damage was centered in the brain.

The damage done by a stroke is usually more localized in the brain than when a brain injury is caused by a major head trauma. Because different parts of the brain control different functions, knowing where the brain has been insulted by the stroke can be helpful in predicting what type of therapy is needed. Knowing where the damage is centered helps doctors and therapists understand the reasons for issues like the loss of speech and motor skills. That does not mean that stroke patients can expect their therapy to be easy or that their post-therapy outcome is assured.

A traumatic brain injury is different from a stroke. A TBI can result in a severe brain scramble that may cause the damage to be less localized. A TBI increases the likely need for several therapies to begin simultaneously. Lots of areas of the brain have been impacted and an MRI is of much less value in determining where to begin.

For those patients who start in a coma, frequent tests are performed to measure their rate of emergence and recovery from that coma. Helen Hayes performs the tests and uses the JFK coma recovery scale. Named after the Johnson Rehabilitation Institution, these simple bedside tests indicate coma patient responses. The scores are used to determine the rate of recovery. These tests also help establish which of the brain's functions may have been most heavily damaged or completely lost in the traumatic injury. The parameters being measured include: auditory response to the ringing of a bell; response to commands to open and close the eyes or move a finger or leg; olfactory senses by placing an ammonia capsule under the nose; tactile awareness by tapping on the shoulders; pain response to a firm pinch; and the patient's vocalization if any. Over the course of time, often weeks, these frequent tests aid the therapy team in planning the program they will use when the patient emerges from the coma. It is a harsh reality that even while the patient is in the coma, the recovery clock is running. Without getting into scoring system details, patients have thirty days to make a six point improvement. Patients who fail to make that improvement are discharged to an uncertain future in a sub-acute facility. A patient scoring six points or more gains an additional thirty days in which to gain another six points. These tests do not take much time to perform. In the first days at a rehabilitation hospital, much of each day is spent by the nursing staff to keep to keep the patient comfortable and quiet.

The goal of all rehabilitation programs is to help each patient reach the highest level of function possible for that individual. That level differs from patient to patient because their injuries and the impact of those injuries are not the same. All involved realize that with TBI patients the outcomes will vary more than with other types of brain injuries.

Months after Angela was strong enough to leave Helen Hayes to continue her recovery in North Carolina, she joined her first support group for brain injury survivors. I attended some of those meetings with her and learned a great deal about the range of outcomes the traumatic brain injured can expect.

Those facilitated sharing discussions were a great way for those recovering from a brain injury to appreciate that others were progressing along the same challenging path that they were traveling. While the road to recovery is a difficult one, survivors who attend these meetings learn that others are also travelling that road. Most areas in the country have brain injury recovery groups and those recovering from a brain injury are encouraged to join and energetically participate in one.

In presentations that the recovering brain injured made and in conversations between them it became quite evident that their permanent losses were indeed varied. For example, I met a man who, seventeen years earlier, had suffered the permanent loss of his ability to taste any food. We had lunch together. He made it very clear that he ate only because he knew he had to eat to live. For all the years since his injury, his devoted and loving wife served him meals with good nutritional balance, but he took little joy from eating.

Others had lost their pre-injury math skills but retained their reading skills; some had lost the reading but kept the math. Some had vision damage resulting in conditions like double vision. Still others suffered personality changes, socialization and behavior problems. Many, likely most, struggle to recover their cognitive skills.

Conversations between TBI survivors often include an exchange of information about how their brain injuries have impacted their lives. All were eager to know the specific areas of loss that Angela had experienced. She never held back in telling them what they seemed to need to know. However, those same conversations usually moved on to other topics. Non-stop talking about their brain injuries must become boring and counter-productive for them.

Happily for TBI survivors, some of their losses are transitory. The changes experienced display themselves soon after the event that injured them but seem to simply disappear or self-correct within days or weeks. Angela had one notable change when she began speaking again. She spoke with the heavy southern accent that she had as a child growing up in Alabama and Florida. Now, years after she had completely lost that accent, it was back but only for a short time. Just as mysteriously as it had appeared, it disappeared on its own. It seemed that the first memories to return were those associated with her youth.

Cognition challenges were a continuing part of Angela's struggle. The term "cognition" was being used all around me but I did not know precisely what it meant and could not picture how it might manifest itself in Angela and others. I had to become informed before writing about it. How could it possibly be treated and overcome? From www.minddisorders.com came a useful definition of cognition: "neuropsychological functioning involved in learning and in basic day to day functioning."

Cognition impairments can include memory loss, poor concentration, loss of focus and attention, poor judgment, difficulty in organizing thoughts or in learning new information, slow thinking and an increased need for simple and specific directions. Several of these were initially difficult for her. For example, she would say something and seconds later repeat that same thing. At times, she would ask if she had already said that and I would tell her that she had. She wanted to know the truth but this condition was one which frustrated her. In a few weeks it did begin to clear itself.

With loss of cognition, therapy is much less certain than for physical therapy where the patient is attempting to re-learn how to control the movement of their body. For some patients, cognition is like a ghost. Sometimes it is there and at other times it is not. Thinking can be clear one moment and fuzzy in the next. Fatigue can be a culprit.

As with all TBI patients, a physician directed Angela's team of therapists. The team used a full range of skills that each had been trained to perform. She had a physical therapist, speech therapist, occupational therapist, social worker, nurse and case worker assigned to her. Their efforts were overseen by a physician. This core team of seven was supplemented by other talent from time to time as needed. The individual members did not rotate on and off her team. She had the same therapists working with her session after session. Working with the same therapy team is important because change and transitions can be difficult for someone with a brain injury.

Between sessions, her therapists exchanged information about how their work with her was progressing. From that exchange, they made adjustments in her regimen. Keeping a team of therapists together is the very best way that they can work effectively to serve the needs of an individual patient.

Each therapy is unique and yet complimentary to the others. Each therapy that Angela needed has a wide variety of tools and techniques from which to select. The tools are important and learning about them allows recovering patients to first appreciate and then to successfully work with their therapists in their individual program. No single set of tools fits every patient equally well; no one-size-fits-all.

Angela needed lots of occupational therapy. She needed to relearn some of the skills required to get on with the job of living. Initially she had difficulty with getting dressed, bathing, eating, and writing.

Next there was speech therapy. It can help with aphasia (loss of the power to use or understand words), proper use of the voice as it recovers, dysphasia (difficult in swallowing) and other cognitive communication issues. Angela needed help here too. Her voice came back but it was a bit more husky and monotone than before the crash. Because of the tracheotomy, she also had problems swallowing.

Physical therapy is one therapy that the general public best understands. It is applied in many situations that have nothing to do with brain injury. Many people have experienced physical therapy themselves or have seen it used with someone they know.

Angela's physical therapy services helped her to re-learn standing, walking and balancing. Her re-learning was necessitated by her brain injury and complicated by the broken C1 vertebra, ribs, collar bone and shoulder she had suffered in the crash. Strengthening and making her neck and shoulder more flexible were a part of her physical therapy.

There was also emotional and psychosocial behavior support. This need could be identified by a social worker or a neuropsychologist. TBI survivors can suffer from anxiety, depression, agitation, isolation, sexuality issues and incidents of downright inappropriate behavior. Sometimes a blend of drugs helps patients accept the interventions of the social worker, but a patient cannot fully recover if left alone with only a bottle of pills.

The patient requires the support of a nurse. Vital signs have to be watched. Blood pressure is key. The nurse also deals with headaches, potential sores from long periods of being confined to bed, surgical wound site healing, refusal or inability to eat, disruption in sleep patterns and a host of other conditions the therapists may not see. Therapists see a patient an hour or so and certainly cannot catch everything. Nurses are a part of the patient's entire day.

In the background but not working directly with the patient is the case manager. From patient intake though discharge, case managers operate as dispassionate patient advocates. I say "dispassionate" because they must maintain a professional level of honest assessment. They must deal accurately and fairly with private insurance payers and government funded programs seeking to pull back on patient coverage before the therapies have had enough time to work. If the payer is pulling back prematurely on coverage, the case manager defends the patient's right to additional time in the program. As the therapy continues, through the use of assessment techniques and proper coding, the case manager tries to convince the insurance company that enough progress is being made to justify continuing coverage. However, if progress is not being made the case manager must acknowledge that fact and begin to make other plans for the patient.

The therapy sessions can be grueling for a TBI survivor. Each therapy requires an hour a day and there are four and sometimes more hours scheduled. Add to the challenge the need for patients to stay on a time schedule and get themselves, often by wheelchair, to their next session. An able-bodied person might not find four hours of these activities to be too demanding, but we are not talking about the able bodied. Therapy is tough work for the patients and there is no other way to describe it.

Exactly one month after her arrival at Helen Hayes, Angela suffered a medical setback. Her halo had come loose from her skull and there were indications of a developing infection where it had been attached. She was returned to Westchester Medical Center where the halo had initially been applied. Angela did not want to go but she knew she must. She spent five days there and lost precious therapy time and momentum.

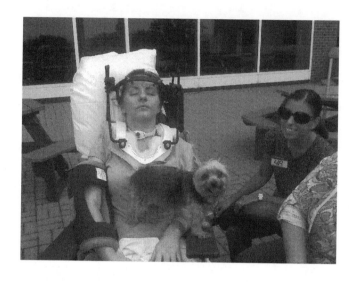

The early days at Helen Hayes

At Westchester the halo was removed, the infected wounds treated and a collar on her neck replaced the halo. They also took a look at her broken bones to see how they were healing. Her broken C-1 vertebra had knitted well enough to make the halo no longer needed. A conventional collar would be enough. That change was welcomed because a patient can deal with a collar so much better than with a halo. Angela certainly did not miss the halo; those who know her thought she already had a permanent one floating above her head.

Angela vividly recalls the round trip by ambulance. Any jostling or bouncing caused her exquisite pain. The ambulance attendant held her hand the whole way. He would say things like, "Angela, we are going to make a turn here and it may hurt. I will tell you when we are about to cross the railroad tracks." She knew he did not have to do any of that; he was simply a compassionate soul. She made a successful effort months later to find out who he was so she could thank him. She wanted to include his name in the book to recognize him. His concern about the HIPAA Patient Privacy regulations caused him to decline her request. He is a wonderful professional.

Concerning her thanking people: at this stage of her recovery, Angela was endlessly reviewing who needed to be thanked and whether they had been. She wondered aloud whether she should do a second or even third round of thanks with each person. Should she give them gifts? Repaying the kindness shown her seemed as though it might never end. It is one of the burdens she created for herself.

Many of those she repeatedly thanked did not feel that a thanks is required. They said things like, "I didn't do that much. I just did what I am supposed to do. It is my job after all; what I am paid to do." They should probably be less modest about what they did for her. While it is their job, these are demanding jobs in a profession that they did not have to choose. Here is an additional consideration for those being given thanks by their patients. In some ways, rejecting the thanks offered is to reject that patient. Therapists and other care-givers should allow themselves to be thanked if the patient is moved to do it.

Angela did not feel guilty about thanking those who have been so helpful to her. As she so insightfully told them, "I was the one in need and you were the giver. From your eyes you see only me. But from my own eyes I see you as one of an army of givers. The enormity of the total gifts given to me is overwhelming."

Angela was also remarkably inquisitive. When entering into a therapy session she wanted to know both the why and the how of what she was expected to do. She was learning as much as she could because she already understood that the day was fast approaching when she would be guiding her own lifelong therapy program.

Before she left their care, her therapy team summarized their experiences with Angela as their patient. They told her they will always remember her as being a recovery-focused hard worker. They acknowledged that she still had visible scars, a droopy eye and face and broken teeth, but they knew she was not going to let her appearance or her ego get in the way of her attempt to recover.

On October 17, Angela was discharged from Helen Hayes two weeks before she had to leave and only ten weeks since the crash. Why did she check out early? Why was Angela in a hurry? She decided that it was time to move to her dad's home in North Carolina. Her therapy would continue but what was the rush to get there? Once there she would have only one of her parents, her dad, helping her. She felt that she would benefit by being in the care of only one, rather than having both continuing to disagree about what was best for her. She needed to be treated as an adult. She felt her father would do that and, for the most part, that turned out to be true. It had also become obvious to some of her therapy team that being surrounded by so many badly brain injured people was not helping her spirits. It was time to go.

Most patients who are recovering from a brain injury hang on at the rehabilitation hospital until their fully allotted time has expired. They are in no hurry to leave because they wish to be as close to perfect as possible when they return to their family and friends. They do not want a stumbling gait or slurred speech to embarrass them upon their return to their usual surroundings. Angela decided that she could deal with those problems once in North Carolina. If she was self-conscious it never showed; it shouldn't have either. Self-consciousness can cause survivors to hide from people who knew them before the injury. Avoiding people prevents the reconnecting that is vital to recovery.

7

Supporting Her Recovery

Strictly speaking, Angela no longer had to be in a rehabilitation hospital; however, she needed lots of care, assistance, therapy and even some out-patient surgical procedures. She needed help with meal preparation and eating (including cutting up food for her), grooming, walking and transportation. She needed to be reminded about her medications and her appointments. She was still in considerable pain and had difficulty sleeping. In other words, she could do little for herself.

Angela had never actually lived in North Carolina. She had gone to a camp there in her youth. She did not really want to go to North Carolina now but go there she must. She was not anywhere near being capable of independent living. Angela loves her dad but had never contemplated living under his roof and being in his care as an adult. He had left her and her little sister many years ago when the Florida divorce was granted. He had not stayed in touch much since. The move was going to be quite an adjustment.

Charlie, her dad, has his home on the side of a mountain in the village of Laurel Park adjacent to Hendersonville, North Carolina. He was providing her a room in that already crowded, small home. With the arrival of Angela and Mair, it would be home to six adults and six dogs as both girls brought their dogs.

Angela's moving in meant Charlie was an on-call chauffer, counselor and medication dispenser. He did not complain of the many demands on his time. When I asked him about having her as his guest, he reminded me that he had lost one daughter, Dayna, and would do whatever it took not to lose his only other child.

Charlie told me that his empathy for Angela's situation was made stronger by his having been severely injured as a young man when he was kicked in the head by a horse. Knocked unconscious, when Charlie awoke he sought no medical attention. He said he had wondered since that time if he had not "lost a little something" from that injury. Every year in our country, thousands of so-called "mild" TBIs go undiagnosed and untreated. The losses those injured people feel are very real.

Mair decided to relocate temporarily to North Carolina and live in that same small home. She hung a curtain across the entrance to the living room; that was

86

her bedroom. She was not about to leave Angela when her need was still so strong. Months later Mair moved away to return to the priorities of her own life. In that length of time, Angela was gaining strength and did not rely upon Mair.

The mountains of western North Carolina are a perfectly wonderful place to live. I can attest to that as my wife and I have lived in these mountains for over twenty years. However, for Angela, Laurel Park was as different from Manhattan as it could be. Laurel Park did have one major advantage at this point in her rehabilitation. It was quiet and picturesque. For her it was one of those "great place to visit but I would not want to live there" locations. She remained a self-described "big city girl." Getting back home to NYC was her objective from the first day she arrived in North Carolina. Her desire to return to the city helped to put a rough timeframe and some recovery urgency before her. Thus, she moved with purpose throughout her North Carolina stay.

It was in North Carolina that I first heard about and then met Angela. I was a member of the Public Relations Association of Western North Carolina. We were told that a young brain-injured woman with a background in public relations wished to come to our meetings. She thought that coming to our monthly meetings was a good way for her to stay connected to the profession she had enjoyed for so many years. Getting out of the house for something other than the usual therapy was an added plus.

In November of 2008, just four months after the crash and her massive injuries, she appeared at our meeting with her dad. She struggled to walk and to stand. Her balance was not yet reliable. The double vision made it worse. She came in on her dad's arm and had a cane in her free hand. Her neck was still in a collar. Her smile was crooked and her speech was halting. Her eyes were not functioning well together and one had a badly drooping eyelid. But she was there and ready to meet people.

Her grit and determination inspired the members of the club. We could see real progress in her recovery from month to month. In language used by her doctors and therapists, when we met she was already on the steep section of a typical S curve recovery.

With the S curve recovery, progress is difficult to see in the first few weeks; obviously none is visible during coma and even into the earliest stages of therapy. Soon however, those headed for some degree of recovery move to the steep and visible section of the S curve. Progress is easy to see in this phase. Then in the final stages, likely sometime into the second year after a TBI, the improvement increments are smaller and more difficult to observe as the S begins to flatten out at the top.

It took me four months to get to know her well enough to make a proposal to her. She and her situation needed to be captured in a book and after the April meeting, I approached and asked if she might allow me to write it. I was confident that my reporting skill would result in my telling her story properly. She had not considered having a book written; the idea was stimulating to her. I gave her a copy of my first book so she and her family could assess my writing capability. After thinking about my proposal for a couple of weeks, she came back with an enthusiastic yes. I was pleased and we soon started planning the project together.

Because she had a lot of recovery work to do, spending time together about the book project fell far down the list. Recovery and the therapy required to achieve it came first. I gathered information on the topic of brain injuries and thought about how her story should be organized and told. The interviews and writing would wait until an appropriate time.

One of the major challenges facing Angela in North Carolina was building a new recovery team. In New York, she had many supportive friends and an established network of doctors and therapists. A new team must be assembled quickly and seamlessly if her recovery was to continue without interruption. She did not want to lose even a little of the ground she had gained.

Once again, Angela found herself fortunate. Her dad's wife, Mary Wall, is a gifted nurse practitioner. In one of those "small world" coincidences, Mary Wall had been the nurse practitioner at the assisted living home in Hendersonville, NC, where my own mother had resided. She took exquisite care of my mother. I knew Angela could get no better care anywhere than she would get from her.

Mary Wall had been at Angela's bedside in New York and was not about to allow any recovery momentum to be lost because she had temporarily relocated to North Carolina. She had a thorough knowledge of the area's healthcare network. She knew many healthcare professionals. She is a bold woman who would not allow Angela to get lost in the system. I asked Mary Wall to describe the system and why it is so difficult for brain injury survivors to get the attention and services that they require.

Here is the essence of what she said. "Brain injury survivors leave the rehabilitation hospital just days or weeks after sustaining their injury. They leave for a home setting (often in a distant city to live with family members) but their healing is far from complete. They usually leave rehab hospitals with cognition problems that make it difficult or impossible for them to manage this transition by themselves. They encounter complexities that include selecting, scheduling, obtaining payment, and providing guidance to their own medical team. By contrast, those recovering from surgery have full use of their brain and can handle their own recovery much more easily. The discharged and newly arriving TBI patient encounters a system that is often already full to capacity and strained by the weight of the paperwork and reimbursement challenges."

In one instance, when Angela needed a surgical procedure, the most qualified doctor had an impossibly busy schedule. His office said the wait would be eight weeks. Mary Wall stepped in and two days later Angela was in his care. Her value in selecting the services Angela needed and getting them started is impossible to overstate.

Angela's therapy file had been referred by Helen Hayes Hospital to CarePartners in Asheville, North

Carolina, twenty miles from her father's home. In this second rehabilitation center she was an out-patient. CarePartners (formerly Thoms Rehabilitation Hospital) provides a wide range of rehabilitation services. The rehabilitation of patients with brain injuries is but one of those.

Angela's new physician and a new therapy team immediately sought to understand the challenges of her case. Valuable recovery momentum must not be lost and would not be. Brain injured people can find it stressful to have to relocate and work with a new team. Angela seemed to take it in stride.

Angela's records from Helen Hayes Hospital were helpful but the new team at CarePartners needed to do its own neuropsychology evaluation of Angela to establish a sound starting point for their therapy efforts. She was, of course, totally supportive of their assessment attempts. More than compliant, she participated energetically.

The head of her program was Edgardo Diez, MD. He gained Angela's confidence quickly and she found him to be very helpful. When we interviewed Dr. Diez, I asked if the physical complications of Angela's case made it more difficult to manage the brain recovery part of the program. Other physicians, outside the CarePartners rehabilitation program, were continuing to perform surgeries to correct problems with her shoulder and her throat.

Her broken right shoulder had been operated on and set at Westchester. As so often happens with complex joints like the shoulder, as it healed it also became more stiff and immobile. Her range of motion was becoming limited. The pain and discomfort kept her from sleeping well. Bone spurs had developed and an audible clicking could be heard when she moved the shoulder. While she did not want any more surgery, she knew she had to have it or risk more pain and loss of use in the future. She had the shoulder bones surgically scraped and the joint cleaned up – a painful operation. But there was good news; now the physical therapy would be more effective. After a few weeks she was pain free and able to fully use that shoulder.

She also needed some correction to the scar that resulted from her emergency tracheotomy. The scar across her throat was visible. She wanted it to be gone, but cosmetic improvement was not the most significant reason for undergoing the procedure. Often when a tracheotomy heals it leaves scar tissue inside the throat. That tissue narrows the throat and can create difficulty in swallowing. She had experienced some of that. More than simply being unpleasant, the scar tissue growing into the throat could become dangerous and choking could result.

The tracheotomy and perhaps the brain injury resulted in changes in Angela's speaking and singing voice. Before the crash she had a beautiful singing voice and she had not been bashful about showing it off to admiring listeners. That singing voice was lost. She had the operation performed on an out-patient basis and the results were what she needed. The visible scar was gone and so was the difficulty in swallowing. She is still waiting for the singing voice to return.

In the crash, her teeth and mouth had suffered significant damage. Some teeth were broken off. She missed being able to flash the smile she had been born to share. Off she went to Hendersonville reconstructive dentist, Dr. Arthur Pearsall. Over the course of many appointments his talent became obvious. At the completion of his work her beautiful smile was back. Her smile and her engaging laugh delighted those around her.

The doctors dealing with the non-brain injury portion of her recovery needed to prescribe medications related to the procedure they performed. Balancing of all these medications can be tricky. Dr. Diez told us that these doctors recognize special issues with a brain injured person. They communicated with him and resolved any important difficulties that could otherwise constitute a setback to the patient. Interaction complications could occur from the use of additional medications, stimulants, dietary supplements, alcohol or medical marijuana a patient might use and fail to report. A brain injured person might not even recall everything that they have taken. Staying on top of these areas can be difficult but is vitally important to the patient's health and recovery.

Dr. Diez stated that the brain tends to establish its own schedule for therapy readiness. Scheduling too much therapy before the brain is ready can frustrate both the patient and the therapy team. Over the years he has suggested to a few patients that they take a brief break from their therapies to allow the brain to catch up. Those breaks can last days or even a few weeks. That approach has been frequently been successful.

Diez's therapy team attempts to re-train the patient's brain while at the same time teaching the patient some strategies needed to compensate. Compensation strategies are critical if portions of the brain do not return to fully functioning capability. Angela understood what he said and identified and refined the use of several strategies to help her accomplish a few tasks that remain difficult and potentially dangerous for her.

The doctor stated that young children and teens do better with recovery from brain injury than adults and much better than the elderly. That is true because young people are still generating new brain cells as a part of their maturing into adulthood.

The brains of adults are no longer growing and their recovery can be tougher. That is why injuries from common occurrences like a fall in the home can be devastating to seniors. Recovery prospects for older patients are less bright if their brain injuries occur after other pre-existing conditions had already developed. For example, those who already suffer from mild dementia simply have less fight left in them. Those who suffer with heart disease, obesity, respiratory problems or diabetes also have little reserves left to fight the brain injury. In no way was the doctor suggesting that older patients they lose hope and give up. He just wants them to know they will have to work harder.

There is also the issue of severity. Obviously, the more severe the brain trauma the more difficult the recovery will likely be. Angela's was severe and had resulted from a one-time incident, the car crash.

However, a succession of minor brain injuries can produce the same result; loss of cognition and other classic symptoms more often resulting from single major traumatic event. Take the example of Cheryle Sullivan, M.D.—one of the survivors that we met along the way. During her informative presentation at a major brain injury conference, this talented physician told how a succession of five minor concussions over the course of her life had ultimately left her unable to perform as a physician.

Her first concussion occurred as a child in a play-related fall. She recalls other instances, over the course of her active outdoor and sporting life, of falling and bumping her head. None of these single incidents required medical intervention at the time they occurred. None of them were of great concern to her – until the last one. It was a minor fall in which the back of her head struck the ground. She was standing on her snow skis at the bottom of the run when her skis slipped forward and she fell. She returned to work but gradually realized that she was not performing as she had been in behalf of her patients. She asked if her medical associates had seen a difference in her, and some admitted that they had. She did the responsible thing and retired.

The point of Dr. Sullivan's story is that a career-ending and life-changing brain injury can happen when a person experiences the last concussive event in a series of seemingly minor events. A major, one-time trauma is not the only way to suffer a life-altering brain injury. See the appendix for information about her book.

Returning to our interview with Dr. Diez, I asked him if a patient's dedication to therapy displayed by the patient made a big difference. He said that it certainly does. Here is example: one of his young patients wanted to learn to drive again. After four years of hard work by the patient and the therapy team, he is safely driving again.

Here is another example. One of his patients is presently five years beyond the date of his injury. He can communicate only by blinking his eyes yet he remains dedicated to enjoying a successful recovery one day. Why does he not give up? Who knows for sure but thankfully he has not. Persistence, grit, determination, dedication, courage, resolve, and faith are all displayed in survivors like this. We need people like this around us because without their example, quitting on ourselves for much lesser reasons (loss of a job, failure in a relationship, back pain, weight gain, you name it) could become epidemic. Brain injured people make great teachers and role models.

Dr. Diez concluded by mentioning that some people see his field as having little personal reward. So many patients will never fully recover. He said that we must remember that he never knew any of his patients personally before they came to him with their brain injury. All he sees is this progress from the first day in his care. Seeing a patient making progress toward their own goals is what he finds rewarding – a real payday for him. This is a doctor who clearly loves his work.

We went to lunch with two of Angela's therapists from CarePartners. Angela's therapy with them had successfully concluded several weeks earlier. These two therapists, with years of experience, were able to provide insight into Angela and the entire practice of therapy for their brain injured clients. Patty Mabe-Parker is a Speech Language Pathologist. Charise Lord is a physical therapist. Here is some of what they shared with us.

Angela was new to them but she was not new to brain injury therapy sessions; she already knew the demands of her therapy routines. As they started with her, they had much of the information they needed. Much of it was provided by a coherent and committed Angela.

Often with a patient just starting out in therapy, the team will seek information from the patient's past in order to better understand what therapy approach might be best to apply. How much formal schooling did the new patient have? How did she do as a student? Did she have any psychological or medical history that might create complications?

With a new patient the team faces a common challenge. If the therapy is to go well, they must first get past the patient's lack of insight into his problem. The patient may initially come across as defiant, non-compliant or negative. New patients are often in denial about their injury. Their behavior seems to reflect their inability to see clearly their own problem and what they must do to overcome it.

After a time, patient depression can set in. Although most of us regard depression as a bad thing, therapists often see it differently. For them it can be a mark of patient progress. The first thought of the patient may be that they are losing ground. In reality, they are becoming aware of what has happened and what it will take to make progress. Depression often results but typically does not persist. As they move beyond depression, their understanding and motivation are stronger and communication channels with therapists are improved.

Angela's therapists described her as a very verbal patient. Many patients can become verbal as they enjoy the encounter and an opportunity to talk. However, since therapists get only an hour a week with each patient, the therapy session must stay on track and not get spent in excessive conversation.

I asked if patients ever seemed to be motivated by a concern that they would disappoint their therapist. Angela chimed in that pleasing her therapist had never crossed her mind. She was doing what she was doing for the right reasons. She was doing her therapy only for herself and for her own recovery. The therapists liked hearing her say that. They added that occasionally patients tried to cover up a lack of progress. But even in those instances the cover-up was not an attempt to please the therapy team. It was more the natural coping and compensating that many people do when interfacing with others.

While in their program, Angela worked very hard. She was heard to say, "Once a TBI always a TBI." Although those words could be an indication of submission to the injury, Angela did not mean them that way. She recognized what was real and true. Her words were a challenge to herself and to her team to keep things moving.

She was more organized and self-directive with her program than many patients are. Therapy regimens can be complex. She had managed complex projects for clients at Hunter PR for years. More than simply a demonstration of her motivation to recover, the reemergence of this personal management skill was yet another indication of her recovery.

Many, perhaps the majority of TBI patients, either do not or cannot manage their own recovery program. If they do not and no family member or friend steps in to direct it, that patient stands a good chance of going to an adult group home or a nursing home. How unfortunate that the absence of a little recovery program management can stop patient recovery.

Angela accepted the reality of not returning to her prior career but she knew that other doors would open for her. Patty and Charise told us how important it is for patients who cannot return to their former line of work to come to grips with their loss of prerequisite professional skills. Patients who were lawyers and doctors seem to have a difficult time with that acceptance. That is easy to understand given their extra years of education investment. Once acceptance finally arrives, as it must, the therapy discussion focuses on "what can I now learn to do?"

Angela had an important question for her two resources. Could she expect to recover her pre-injury emotional age. She had attended a camp for people with brain injuries called Camp Carefree. A fellow camper was a man of about forty-five. To Angela he had seemed more like a boy of twelve. His approaches and come-ons to her had not been age appropriate and she had recognized it. Both therapists said that it is impossible to generalize but that they had seen no indication that Angela would be emotionally stuck at age thirty for the rest of her life. If future life experiences allow for emotional development, patients are very likely to develop accordingly. This is one more good reason for a brain injured person to seek new experiences and challenges.

I asked the therapists some specific questions about Angela. Had she ever had a bad day in therapy? They answered with a yes. One day she came in for a scheduled session and had forgotten to bring her completed "Mind Bender" homework assignment. She was extraordinarily stressed about having failed to remember. The therapists knew that her many indications of being stressed meant the session they had planned to conduct was not going to work. Not wanting to waste a precious day of Angela's limited time in their program, they decided to work on exercises to reestablish her calmness: breathing, balance and slow movements. The change they made in the session for that day worked well. What she was shown has helped her since in dealing with those days when her schedule is full and she feels herself failing to get tasks completed as planned. She is able to deal with stress better.

In the CarePartners program, Angela had some victories. She had significant problems maintaining her balance. A fall could result in a loss of progress in therapy or worse. Her therapists knew the balance problem was one that they could help her correct. Physical therapist Charise created some training exercises specifically for Angela. After using the exercises and just five months after the crash, she was able to take her first unassisted shower – a personal victory.

Some patients had different and more difficult challenges. They had sequencing problems with actions like knowing to turning the water on once they were in the shower. Some did not recognize the functional difference between a body washing brush and a tooth brush. These challenges could be overcome with dedication to their therapy.

As we finished our excessively large lunch (what most restaurants seem to serve these days) I asked about patient nutrition and weight gain or loss. Frankly, Angela was gaining weight and she did not seem to notice that she was. At least, if she did notice, she never mentioned it.

The two therapists said that patients may not recall eating lunch and may have a second lunch as a result. Also, changes in metabolism and some medications can exacerbate weight changes. Additionally, if the brain injury involved the hypothalamus area of the brain, one patient may want to eat all the time while another patient may have no appetite at all. Weight gain seems to happen more often than weight loss. It is likely that many TBIs would benefit from the help of a nutritionist.

Our final CarePartners interview was with Tina Lipscomb, Patient Access Coordinator. An experienced nurse, Tina is also a compassionate and delightful person. She possess the skills and personality traits important needed to keep insurance payments coming so that the patient can stay in the program long enough to make progress. As her case manager, Tina worked successfully in Angela's behalf.

Our day of interviews was over and we headed home. Angela had sat through all the interviews, asked excellent questions, and offered helpful input from a TBI survivor's point of view. She was, after all, the only brain injury survivor in the conversation. When we stated something incorrectly she jumped in with a helpful correction or clarification. On the way back home, Angela said she knew why the name CarePartners fit the organization so well. She said that was exactly what they were to her: care partners.

Angela's ability to participate during the interviews had improved significantly since the interviews conducted during our trip to New York just a few months earlier. This improvement was one more sign of her recovery. These signs of progress were important for her to be aware of. I always told her about evidence of progress once it became clear that it was real and consistent. Others were surely doing the same. She thrived on the input and always made an entry into her journal about it. Angela, the trained writer, made great use of her journals.

A brain injured person needs more than therapists and physicians to make progress toward recovery. For anyone on the road to recovery, friends are vital too. Many friends were waiting in North Carolina like the members of the Public Relations Association who accepted her so warmly. Most were new friends, people who knew of her through her family but yet to meet her. Angela was not shy about making new friends.

She was also good about staying connected to friends and followers all over the country. She enthusiastically posted updates on the personal page Mair had established for her on the Caring Bridge web site. Old friends and other interested people could check in to see what she was thinking and doing. This online circle of friends, most not likely to ever meet her, took heart in her reports. Some were brain injured themselves or were helping a brain injured person through recovery. When she could have easily justified sticking to her own recovery, she constantly reached out through Caring Bridge and in meetings with brain injury survivors to share her experience and to offer them her help.

Her posting of those updates provided her with an early challenge; to post them she first had to write them. Angela had a talent for and a love of writing. Her brain injury made writing much more challenging. However, facing and overcoming important challenges is critical to the recovery process. Writing to others interested in her status was a welcomed challenge. She repeatedly heard from those following her progress just how inspired they were by what she had to say. Her spirit was keeping many others from giving up on themselves. She was giving them a generous gift.

Supportive friends also came to North Carolina to visit with Angela. One of the first to arrive was her longtime hair stylist, Simone Sanchez. She had styled Angela's hair in Manhattan for years but had moved to Atlanta well before the crash. Upon discovering that Angela was in rehab in North Carolina, she made the four-hour drive to provide her with a complimentary cut and style. It was Angela's first professional cut and style since the crash. She had not lost her desire to look well groomed. She needed and wanted a nice styling and her friend delivered it.

Calvin Dennison came too. Redwood Creek Wines was a Hunter PR client and Angela managed the account. Cal was the brand's winemaker and her client contact. They had travelled to many cities together. She had written marketing material and speeches for him to use with Redwood distributors. When he heard of her injury, he felt a strong need to visit and see how she was doing. Cal had a special understanding of what she might be facing. His wife had experienced a traumatic brain injury in a horse-riding accident years earlier. When he took Angela to lunch, he saw early signs of her recovery and left greatly encouraged. Cal said he had become a friend of Angela in the same way that he suspected others had. He was drawn to her.

Permit me to use magnets as an analogy. Those who have held two magnets in their hands know that when the poles are properly aligned the magnets are held together by powerful forces. However, by changing the alignment, the magnets strongly repel each other. Sadly, some brain injured persons never achieve the proper alignment and drive friends away, without that intention. Others, like Angela, position themselves properly and attract and hold friends. Angela is a friend magnet.

Another who joined her recovery team was Alicia Knighten. Alicia knew Angela's dad from her involvement with a music festival he had helped organize and manage for several years. Alicia knew Charlie was not flush with money and that unanticipated expenses like the trips to New York were straining his available funds. Alicia organized a benefit featuring performances of many musicians from this region. When the local musicians learned of her injury and the family's financial need they willingly donated their time. A local businessman donated the use of his music theater space. The show raised several thousand dollars to help cover family expenses. Once again, complete strangers had come together to do the right and generous thing.

The folks in North Carolina were giving their all to Angela. She appreciated every kindness and was sure to tell them so. She had come as a guest and had received the southern hospitality she knew about from having lived in Alabama and Florida as a youngster. At the same time, from the day of her arrival she had not seen herself staying forever. She knew where her home was meant to be. She knew where she would start her new life.

8

Saying Good-bye "Life One"—Hello "Life Two"

In August, 2009, just a year after the crash, Angela felt physically and emotionally strong enough to return for a one week visit to New York City. She needed to see if she was capable of navigating in the city where she had lived and worked for eight years. This "trial run" would determine when and even if she would one day be able to return to live there.

Since the crash, she had been back to the city only once. She had flown in for a two-day meeting in mid-June. Hunter had obtained her airline tickets and had made all the arrangements for her visit. They took good care of her.

Every summer, Hunter PR has something euphemistically called "Hunter Community College." This off-site meeting has team building as one of it focal points. Angela was invited because they still regarded her as a member of the team. From all accounts, she

111

more than held her own during the meeting by asking questions and making suggestions that helped make the meeting a success.

Angela loved being back among her old friends from work. She went with the intention of being a contributor during the meeting and she was. She had not gone to be a distraction or the center of attention. When the meeting ended, she flew right back to North Carolina. This trip was a good early test of her ability to participate in a meaningful group activity and of her travel skills. She passed this first solo travel experience, with some help on departure and arrival, and deservedly felt good about it.

Eight weeks after that two day trip, she was ready for a much more challenging trip to New York City. I volunteered to drive her there. This time she made all the detailed arrangements and set the daily schedule for both of us. It was an involved trip and had many more objectives than the June trip. In handling this task with its multiple objectives, destinations and meetings just weeks after the first trip, she demonstrated a major improvement in her planning capability. Yet another critical life skill had returned. She deserved to be thrilled and she was.

Prior to this trip, my time with Angela had been in one or two hour increments. From time to time I had provided local transportation to relieve her dad. He spent countless hours driving her somewhere and waiting there to take her home. I took her to therapy sessions or to one of our book-prep interviews. Each of these ended for me when I dropped her off at her dad's house, just five minutes up the mountain from my own home. When she left my car and entered his home, my responsibilities ended and his, once again, began. These short sessions were easy for me. Our trip together to New York would be different in duration and intensity.

She had important and unfinished business to do there. Much of that business had to do with seeing former co-workers, friends from the city, friends from the neighborhood in Putnam Valley that she and Rich had known only four months before the crash, the doctors, nurses and therapists at Helen Hayes hospital and Rich's parents and sister. For weeks she planned every detail of the trip.

She had become absolutely convinced that she needed to go. Her doctors and therapists seemed to think she was up to it. We were already in the research and interview phase for the writing of her story. The trip would give me more contacts and background information. We both had reasons to go.

The trip started on Sunday morning. I picked her up for a thirteen-hour drive to her home in Putnam Valley, NY. On the dashboard of my car sits a small, plastic green frog. I keep it there for luck. When Angela saw the frog she smiled. As it turns out, she is crazy about frogs and was thrilled that I had brought one along. The presence of that frog was, for her, a reassuring symbol with which to begin our trip.

She handled the long ride very well. She napped only once along the way. With physical problems like her stiff shoulder, persistent double vision and very little stamina, it must have been the adrenaline that kept her awake, thinking and talking. We were locked into a non-stop conversation. She poured out her memories and her soul. Perhaps the stimulation came from knowing where we were headed. I tried to keep her comfortable by letting her share what she chose to without prying. We talked about what she wanted to talk about.

Several times along the way something would come to her that she had not been able to recall since the injury. After sharing it with me, I could hear her softly say "Wow! That's a memory." Those words were spoken in a celebratory manner. She was verbalizing how it felt to recover. It was like watching a child open presents at Christmas. Her joy was that real. Happily, she would experience many more "Wow" moments in the months to come.

As we drove along, more and more memories came flooding back. Some were large and significant. Others were small and just fun to relive. One she talked about in full-color detail was a romantic weekend she and Rich had enjoyed. As he drove along he would not tell her where they were headed. Angela was crazy with anticipation. He had secretly planned a weekend at the Saugerties lighthouse, located on the Hudson River at the mouth of Esopus Creek. This operational lighthouse is also the site of an intimate and unique bed and breakfast. As luck would have it, they were the only guests registered for that weekend.

She recalled the walk through the dark required to reach the lighthouse and their accommodations there. Rich had not been a Boy Scout; he was a product of big city suburbs. His imagination on that dark walk through the woods included man-eating animals just waiting to pounce on them. Angela thought it hysterically funny. They held hands and shared laughs as they walked.

She remembered that weekend, yet other more significant times with Rich were not there for her. For example, as much as she loved him, she cannot recall anything about their wedding day. She sincerely wants to but cannot. When she looks at the photo album of the wedding she sees people clearly celebrating; however, she cannot remember the happy occasion captured in the photos. She cannot make an emotional connection to the event. The photos seem to be from someone else's life. So what? She is no less a caring and loving person for lack of perfect recall. I told her that in as reassuring a way as I could find the words to say it.

As Angela and I talked about memory loss, we concluded that she has three categories of lost memories. First are those she believes must be remembered and will return in time. Her wedding day is in that category. However, Angela has a rational way of understanding and, for now, accepting the loss of that memory. She believes that Rich is watching over her from heaven and that as soon as he sees that she is ready he will shepherd her through the process of getting those wedding memories back.

Angela is a spiritual person. However, she does not wait endlessly for messages from beyond before she sets a plan and acts on it. She keeps moving forward. However, if she does see a sign that she is on the right path she is reassured by it. She believes, as do I, there is nothing wrong with seeking and accepting help from willing and interested spirits.

The second category of memories includes those memories she would enjoy regaining but do not fit the "must recall" category. They could help her understand who she is and how she got to be who she is. An example would be her lost childhood memories. She can go on living without them and may have to, but their return would be helpful.

A third category are those lost memories that would be nice to recover but whose permanent loss would be okay. She could easily live with their loss. One of these was Rich's favorite meal. She seems to recall that he had a favorite but cannot recall what it was.

Identifying these three categories seemed to unburden her. She realized that every memory is not of equal importance. She could sort them out into these categories and take her time in regaining those she felt most strongly about.

It was interesting to hear what she does recall and how she reports it. Almost every memory she has is a happy one. I have no sense that she was denying or filtering her less than happy memories. It simply seemed that the happy ones out-numbered and drowned out the noise of the unhappy ones. It is a wonderful way to be and also helpful to the healing of her mind and body.

I reassured Angela about what memory loss is and how all of us experience it to some extent. My effort was not to make her feel better about losing her memories. It was to have her understand that she is not alone in her memory losses—we all walk that common ground.

Just how important are all these memories anyway? Brain injured persons, sometimes too strongly urged on by others, can create lots of frustration for themselves, adding stress that is not helpful in attempts to heal. Trying too hard to remember the past could also cause the brain injured person to focus too much on the past. Angela expressed a desire and intention not to try too hard or too long to regain memories that simply were not there.

As I drove along, I noticed that she was not nervous about being out on the Interstate highways with heavy traffic and big trucks. Had she been nervous about the ride it would have been completely understandable. She did, however, after several hours on the road, compliment my driving; she appreciated my habit of maintaining a safe distance between my car and the vehicles around me. Thus, I knew that she was aware of the risks of highway travel but was unafraid.

Preparation for the trip included buying snacks to eat in the car; one of those was a package of Rich's Cinnamon Scones, a random purchase. When Angela saw the label she believed it to be another indication that her own Rich was looking out for her and sending messages like the label on the scones package to reassure her that he was. I felt exactly the same way and told her so. We did not dismiss the label on those scones as a coincidence.

We found little things that kept happening were re-enforcing to us on our mission. They continued to occur all during this trip and since. Were they happening more often or are we just more accepting of their ongoing presence in our lives? Was I getting carried away or just becoming sensitive to what I had missed for far too many years in the rush of my own life? Angela became my eyes, ears and nerve-endings. She restores awareness and sensitivity to those around her.

Before this trip, I had never been responsible for anyone who had suffered a TBI. Now I was heading for NYC with my young charge. It had been little more than a year since her devastating injury. We knew that this trip would be full of emotional moments and physical demands for her. As I look back on it now and as I have come to know her much better, I am not surprised that she did so well on this trip. I remain surprised that I did.

After a long drive we finally arrived at Angela's home. It was well after dark and we had some difficulty getting the door unlocked. Once inside, we discovered that an earlier basement water problem had caused the closed-up home to become quite damp. We opened a few windows and retired to our bedrooms to get some sleep.

When the first light of Monday morning came into my room I was up and out. Angela had told me that I just had to have bagels and coffee from the little coffee shop in the village. Aptly named, Simply Bagels, it had been a favorite of hers during the four months they had lived in Putnam Valley. Breakfast required only a quick stop on the fifteen minute drive to the commuter train station in Peekskill. From Peekskill it was a one hour ride to the city. From door to door, the commute was about ninety minutes in and ninety minutes out each day, but she thought it was worth it to have a quiet home of their own.

I drove the two miles into the village to the bagel shop, drank my coffee and then ordered a bagel sandwich and coffee to take back to Angela. While drinking my coffee, I recorded my thoughts about the trip and the interviews in a spiral notebook. By staying at the shop to drink my coffee, she had the private time she needed to get ready for the day.

Every morning that week I returned for another combination of ingredients in a bagel sandwich with coffee. Her medications could not be swallowed on an empty stomach. Doctor's orders—not mine.

By Thursday morning the young man behind the counter was so curious that he asked what I was doing during my visit to their village. I told him and the other employees about Angela's injury and other losses that she had suffered. I told them how much they and their bagels and coffee had meant to Angela when she moved into the village just over a year earlier. In an unexpected act of kindness and concern, they sent the order with their compliments and their best wishes for her recovery. This was yet another of those small kindnesses that came her way from so many people.

After Monday's breakfast we were on our way to Helen Hayes Hospital. The day of our visit , August 31, 2009, was exactly thirteen months after the crash and just ten months since her discharge from Helen Hayes. She had arranged to have two of her dear friends from college days there too. We met Jennifer Murphy and Bernadette Mahoney in the parking lot and happily moved toward the lobby entrance . They both lived down the Hudson more than an hour away: Jennifer in the city where she is a practicing psychologist and Bernie in metro New Jersey. She really wanted to see them while in the area. She also felt she might need some emotional support that day that only old girlfriends could provide. It was her first visit to the hospital since being discharged.

Happy to return—but as a visitor

Angela had a huge smile on her face. She confidently walked in from the visitor's parking lot and into the massive lobby where she easily and unemotionally recalled facility features of the building and grounds. Leading us across the first floor to the elevator, she offered a memory from her stay with almost every step. Once in the elevator she spotted one of her therapists and called out his name, Dave.

He did not immediately recognize her so Angela reintroduced herself. She reminded him that he had been the first person assigned to take her out for lunch at a local restaurant several weeks into her rehab. She said it was one of the best times of her post injury life – just to get away from the hospital for an hour or so. He was pleased to be remembered.

Exiting the elevator on the fourth floor, we headed for the brain injury recovery unit. We had previously obtained the consent of the hospital public relations department to conduct interviews for this book. The unit knew we were coming that morning but not exactly when we would be there. The air was crackling with anticipation. Angela's nurse, Barbara Whalen, was the first to see Angela coming down the corridor. She called out to people working around the unit, "Hey everyone, here comes Angela." The reunion party was on. The whole team instantly formed into one big hug-ball with Angela in its center. For the first time in over a year she saw the faces of her recovery team. Their names came back to her easily too. She called out to them.

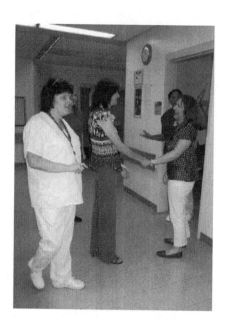

A reunion with the Helen Hayes team

Angela's returning for a visit to thank the staff was not the norm. As we heard later that day, after they are discharged, brain injured patients rarely return to the unit to personally thank those who had worked so hard with them. I asked why so few returned and got a very sensible answer. Most former patients simply wish to forget the place and move on. Returning was a real downer and maybe even a mild emotional set-back. The rare return of a recovering patient seemed to act as therapy for the therapists. Seeing Angela doing so well seemed to reassure them of their personal and collective worth to those whose lives they work so hard to restore.

Several hours of one-on-one interviews were scheduled with members of her therapy team. As was our intent, I did a major portion of those interviews without having Angela in the room. That way I could ask questions about her that her therapists might find difficult to answer candidly with her sitting right there. She understood that and waited patiently outside the room. Angela was invited back in once those questions had been handled.

I entered into the interviews with the idea that these therapists were "heroes of healing." When the therapists heard me use that term, they were quick to correct my thinking. They did not see themselves as heroes. They kept insisting that they were "just doing their jobs." I honored their requests and stopped addressing them as heroes but told them there was more to what they did than "just doing a job." Some jobs might adequately be described with those words; providing therapy for brain injured people is not one of those jobs.

We will start with my interview with Barbara Whalen. She had been a nurse for forty-one years. In that time she had done it all; medical surgery, home care, and public school nursing. She had been at Helen Hayes for the past nineteen years. After sixteen years there, hospital management asked her to consider a move to the traumatic brain injury unit.

Barbara told us that moving into the brain injury unit had been a difficult decision for her as it had been for many others over the years. While she knew that there were many positive outcomes for patients who went through the unit, she also knew that some could not be helped. She had a particularly hard time dealing with the very young. After prayerful thought, she took the position and had served the brain injured for three years. She loved the work and her patients.

Barbara offered these observations about the unit and the work there. She said that working as a team is an absolute imperative. There cannot be a pecking order that allows one member of the team to call the shots or set the priorities for the patient. Every patient needed to be managed on a time schedule so that all the medical and therapeutic treatments could be achieved. However, as the demands of each day played out, everyone had to be somewhat flexible. At the end of the day, the patient always had to come first.

She emphasized that it is not acceptable to judge the risks a patient had taken that resulted in their brain injury. All patients are served without prejudice. For example, while rock climbing was not something she would ever do or recommend to others, a brain injured rock climber deserved to be dealt with non-judgmentally. What had landed patients in this situation had nothing to do with what they needed once injured.

Many team members had a tender or funny memory of Angela. Barbara told me one. In order to gauge whether a patient's cognitive recovery is occurring, she and others repeatedly ask simple questions: What year is this? What day is this? Where are you now? Having responded successfully to these questions often and applying her sense of humor to the situation, Angela answered one day, "Why are you asking? Don't you know?" She knew the answers yet understood why the questions had to be asked.

The next team member interviewed was Angela's occupational therapist, Kimberly Reynolds. Angela also worked some with student intern Kimberly Robinson. Occupational therapy is not intended to teach a brain injured person a skill like welding or carpentry. An occupational therapist prepares a brain injured person with the life skills needed to survive outside the hospital.

In shaping the patient's program, therapists check for any measureable deficits in attention, memory, problem solving and also note important insights the patient may have about himself. With those deficits and insights as a backdrop, they teach life-sustaining (i.e. occupational) skills like bathing, dressing, grooming, cooking, eating and other necessary self-care and survival skills.

The occupational therapist described the key similarities and differences between a stroke patient and a traumatic brain injured patient. She works with both.

As they enter initial rehabilitation, both the stroke and the TBI patients get an hour a day of each of the three main types of therapy. Occupational, speech and physical therapies move in parallel until an assessment of the individual patient suggests a need to re-balance the time spent on each. If a patient needs more speech therapy, time is deducted from one of the other therapies less needed by that patient. The outcome for both stroke and TBI depends on the initial severity of the injury and many other factors.

Stroke patients appear more physically intact. TBI patients often show up for their first sessions still showing lacerations, bruises and bone breaks.

Stroke patients seem to have more insight as to the losses they have suffered. However, better insight does not necessarily mean better acceptance of their situation. Neither does that insight determine the completeness or timeliness of their recovery.

If given her choice occupational therapist Kim would prefer to work with TBI patients. They are a tremendous challenge and tend to present a wider array of post event needs. After several years in the field, she is fascinated by how the brain works to heal itself. She regards herself as a facilitator and an advocate for her patients. Often she wishes she had more than the six to eight weeks she gets with patients before insurance coverage runs out and they must leave for the less rigorous out-patient therapy programs. She knows that eight weeks is precious little time to regain the all-important cognitive skills (perception, memory, judgment) that patients have lost.

She made another significant point. Some patients were limited in some way before their TBI. Pre-existing limitations are not likely something a therapist can change. For example, Angela had never been really strong in mathematics. To expect her to demonstrate a skill she never had can frustrate both the patient and the therapists. Background information about the patient is of real importance to a therapist but can be difficult or impossible to acquire from the patient. This is where a family member or close friend can be most helpful. An honest reporting of what has always been true of a brain injury survivor can jump-start the therapy and save precious time.

Another role of the therapy team, especially the occupational therapist, is the training of the family members or others who will be providing support when the brain injured person leaves the rehab hospital. That training teaches technique and the psychology of its application. The patient may be mostly or exclusively in the care of family members after discharge. Unless the family commits to some training in providing care to their brain injured family member, the patient will not progress well. The patient and the untrained family will become frustrated or even hostile toward each other.

Even with training, providing support at home will not be easy but the results will be better. Family members of patients are welcomed to attend any therapy session given to their own TBI patient. By watching, they see more clearly what they need to do and exactly how to do it right. Some families seek an abundance of such training while others show no interest and commit no time.

Tara Hoffman was with Angela's speech therapist. Angela refers to her as "one tough cookie." One day when therapy was scheduled, nurse Barbara, herself no push-over for patients, was about to allow a tired and perhaps a little dispirited Angela to skip the therapy sessions scheduled for that day. Had Tara been less dedicated to her patients she could have accepted that news and had a free hour to herself. Not Tara! She went directly to Angela's room and asked her if she would "sleep on the job if she were back at work at Hunter PR." Angela said, no, she would not sleep even as she pointed out that her boss Jon at Hunter PR took naps on the job. Tara reminded her that therapy was now her job and that sleeping was not doing that job. Before Angela could say, "let's do it," the speech therapy session was underway. Sometimes a therapist has to challenge, perhaps even shame, a patient to get her going.

Tara helped me to understand all that was involved with speech therapy. It is much more than learning to talk properly. In Angela's case it also involved teaching her to swallow. Her emergency tracheotomy had left scar tissue at the site of the procedure. The problem was more critical than simply having difficulty in swallowing. Because Angela could easily aspirate food or fluids into her lungs, there was real urgency in teaching her how to successfully swallow. It would be awhile before an operation would surgically remove the scar tissue. (It was removed weeks later in an out-patient procedure after Angela returned to North Carolina.) Meanwhile, she had to learn to eat, drink and swallow while at Helen Hayes. It could have been a matter of life and death for her.

Tara was like several of Angela's therapists at Helen Hayes, and in other rehab locations, who had not always been in a therapy profession. She had studied psychology and started her career in that field. Later, a member of her own family had required speech therapy. Tara felt that the loss of one's ability to speak had to be the worst loss anyone could suffer. When she saw what speech therapy was all about and what a difference it had made for her family member, she changed careers. To hear Angela tell it, Tara has the gift that all patients need and she gives it freely.

Physical therapist Tammy Goedken had also started in another professional field and left it to train as a therapist. After being a chemist for seven years, she realized that she was not cut out for the isolation of bench work in a chemistry lab. She took the training required to become a physical therapist and became a gifted one.

Tammy shared some vivid details about her time working with Angela. While mastering the tools and techniques required of a physical therapist, she also had an excellent sense of what it takes to enjoy success with her patients. She connects well with the soul and spirit of her patients.

She said that a therapist never knows for sure if a new patient will ever walk again until that patient takes his first step. After that wobbly first step, the next steps can be a precursor as to how well he will eventually walk. Each of those first steps seems like a marathon to the patient.

She further said, "everyone wants to walk." I asked her if it might be possible that every patient starts by saying to her that he wants to walk but has yet to understand the difference between saying it and actually doing it. She agreed, based upon her experience, that until the patient understands the work and the pain involved neither he nor the therapist can know with certainty. Wanting to walk again is not going to make it happen; work may. However, it is not possible to look at patients badly twisted and lying in bed and predict how they will do in therapy. Some who appear to be unlikely to walk produce surprisingly good results.

Patients have a highly personal concept of what post injury "walking" means to them. Some may mean dependent walking in which case someone is alongside to brace or hold them up. Others may mean walking alone in some form of exercise like hiking. She has to work with them through a few sessions to discover what they mean.

In actual clinical measurement there are two definitions that the case worker uses with the insurance provider to describe a patient's progress in relearning to walk.

First, "household" distances walking means the patient rehabilitated can safely move within the confines of his own home. At "household" distances the insurance company will allow the patient to be discharged and then to be given therapy in the home; it may not be quite as effective as the therapy done in a rehab hospital but still well worth doing. Therapy at home is more difficult because the visiting therapist works without an assistant and without slings and other equipment.

Physical therapy delivered in the home does have some advantages for the therapist. The therapist gets to see the patient in action in his own surroundings – the patient's real world. It also presents and opportunity to discover the level of involvement of the patient's family.

A second and higher level of therapeutic success is defined as "community ambulator." These patients can leave home and, as the name implies, walk around the community. While this level of patient accomplishment is desirable it is not always possible.

It is rare for a patient to make absolutely no progress after thirty days of therapy. Sometimes a new medical complication slows progress. Or in the case of a TBI, so much cognition may be lost that a patient simply cannot follow the instructions. Yet it is likely that even months later cognition may markedly improve and physical therapy can begin afresh and produce great results.

Depression is a very common reason for a patient's lack of responsiveness to the challenge. A full array of drug mixes can help but they can take two to four weeks to ramp up and become effective. Angela, while not depressed, did need a drug to help her stay awake.

Tammy knows that to be successful with her brain injured patients she must not argue with them. Nor can she treat them as children. Instead, she manipulates them "in a good way" to get results. For example, early in one of their therapy sessions, Tammy challenged Angela to "take four steps." She was surprised when Angela responded, "I hear that and will raise it to eight." That is so like Angela as Tammy joyously reported.

Tammy discovered that Angela loved to sing. Her singing voice had been damaged by the tracheotomy procedure the night of the crash. Though no longer able to sing as she once had, the patient and the therapist still found themselves harmonizing on a song titled "Angel from Montgomery." That song means a lot to Angela because she and her guitar-playing father had sung it for years. He played it for her while she was still in the coma and again after she emerged from it. Therapy sessions are hard work for the patient and for the therapist. A few light moments spent in song can make them more tolerable for both.

One more story simply must be told concerning the day of her return visit. Before leaving the fourth floor Angela, with permission from the staff, returned to "her room." A twenty-two year old woman occupied the room on the day of the visit. After graduation from college with a double major in math and English, this young woman had surgery for the removal of a brain tumor. A benign tumor was successfully removed, but some brain tissue was damaged. Sadly, this collateral, surgical damage does occur. Unfortunately, while it saved her life, this corrective surgery completely disrupted her cognition. She would need a lot of therapy to regain it.

The patient's mother was in the room attending to her daughter as she had been for most of each day. She was obviously devastated by her daughter's condition. In her typically spirited fashion, Angela entered the room to introduce herself. She told the young patient and her mother that the girl was in the "lucky bed" – the bed from which Angela had escaped one year earlier. She reassured them that the girl could and would do the same thing. Before leaving she took the mother aside and quietly reassured her that, based upon Angela's personal experience, she knew that the lives of both the mother and her daughter had been changed forever. She told her not to lose hope and that her role was of vital importance to her daughter. Her quick visit raised their spirits. That visit also showed that Angela's lifelong talent for lifting others had not been lost to her own brain injury. Her future career as an advocate for brain injured people was taking shape.

The day went quickly and left us short of time to meet with others on Angela's team, but one must be identified. Dr. Glenn Selinger, the boss or leader of the team, is the Director of Traumatic Brain Injury Rehabilitation and is a board certified Neurologist. He was busy as usual during the work day; putting patients first meant not being able to see us. We understood, of course, but do wish to thank him for his dynamic leadership. Dr. Selinger's staff describes him as a "great guy," and he must be.

In our interviews we noted a significant cloud hanging over the therapy team. Funding needed to treat the brain injured is drying up. That could mean less time available to each patient even as the total number of patients is growing. For example, Helen Hayes hospital had seen a reduction in state funding and had been forced to declare a hiring freeze. State funding is crucial because so many of the hospital's patients are funded by Medicare and Medicaid.

Helen Hayes has also seen an increase in the number of returning military personnel with traumatic brain injuries. The relative proximity of Helen Hayes to West Point explains part of that increase. Yet the hospital could be forced to turn away some injured veterans or ration the availability of therapists because of funding cuts and hiring freezes. Brain injuries to our military veterans bring increased public attention and pressure for proper funding for brain injury research and treatment.

We left Helen Hayes to have a very late lunch with Angela's girlfriends, Jen and Bernie, at a local diner. All four of us reflected on the day we had just spent. There was much to celebrate together. Angela had anticipated a possible need for their emotional support during the day. That need never emerged but she was grateful to these old friends for giving up another day of their lives to help her put her own life back together. After lunch there were hugs in the parking lot. They turned south toward the city and we turned north to go a few miles up-river to her home in Putman Valley. It had been quite a day.

That evening, seeing her neighbor Bob DeSantis, Angela yelled across the back fence to him. She asked him to come over for a visit and to meet with me. She told him, as she would tell others over the weeks and months ahead, that I would be writing a book about her and about all the wonderful people who had helped her along the road to recovery. She told him that he would be named in the book. He was humbled by the news.

It turned out that Bob had been a physical therapist for many of the early years of his work life. He knew more than a little about brain injuries, having worked with scores of people who had suffered them. Twenty years earlier had made a career change. He became a painter employed at Saint John's Regional Hospital and steward of the painter's union there.

I asked about Bob's first impressions of the young couple who had moved in next door. He said he thought they were very special. Richard was a really nice guy. Angela liked his garden and was envious of his Jacuzzi.

He knew they were going to be good neighbors and a nice addition to this close knit community.

Bob remembers the night Rich was killed and Angela so badly injured. Weeks earlier, Rich had given Bob a copy of the CD he had recorded. Ironically Bob had listened to it for the first time in the early evening the night of the crash. He and other neighbors did not find out about what had happened until Angela's friends came out from the city to check on the pets. Once the word got out it spread quickly. People in the neighborhood wanted to help.

Bob and his family were very helpful after the crash. For weeks they prepared and delivered hot meals to Angela's family when they returned to the home after another arduous day at the hospital. Bob had kept an eye on the place and brought in tradesmen to fix any problems he found. For example, the boiler needed repair and he got it done.

I asked Bob, now that he was seeing her again after a year, how he thought Angela was doing in her recovery effort. He thought for a moment and said he knew it would be a long road but that he believed she had a great chance to make it. He was impressed by her attitude and saw that she was a fighter. Bob said, "You have to have you." He meant that unless a patient is committed to himself there is no hope.

My inclination was to categorize Bob as a hero and I told him so. He was puzzled and rejected the suggestion immediately. He said, and I will never forget it, "Aren't we all just supposed to help each other?"

Tuesday brought other interviews with neighbors. Our meeting with someone Angela had tagged as "the pool lady" was memorable. Irene Setton had grown up in the valley and had never left it. She had been a Floridan home owner for the past thirteen years. Angela and Irene had met only twice before the crash. Once they had exchanged the "hello, how are you" greeting. The second time was at the estate's private swimming pool during an early season, all-neighbor cook-out. As a long term resident, Irene could have stuck to her established friends and allowed Angela to sit alone or to force her way into new contacts. Instead, Irene introduced Angela to everyone, gave her a margarita and got to know her.

Irene told us that since the crash she had made a daily habit of walking past Angela's empty home and saying a prayer for her recovery. My guess is that others were doing that too. She had frequently checked for any news posted on the Caring Bridge internet account established while Angela was deeply comatose. Many people from the neighborhood and around the country followed her progress on those pages.

Irene made several other observations. Although it was still early in the recovery process, I asked her what she could imagine was within the range of future possibilities for Angela. Irene said she could "imagine Angela would move back to Manhattan, find meaningful employment and fall in love again." You should have seen the smile on Angela's face. Irene believes that people who have suffered a personal tragedy often become better people than they were before that tragedy. Seeing what was happening with Angela, I found her point to be valid and touching.

Late Tuesday morning Angela and I walked around her old neighborhood. It was a warm and sunny day. She led the way for a short hike on one of the trails that she and Rich had enjoyed in their four months in the Floridan community. Walking through the neighborhood, we met and had pleasant exchanges with former neighbors. Many of them had heard about her but had not had time to get to know her. It was a little awkward when some of them said things like, "I never expected to see you today," when they may really have meant, "I never expected to see you ever again." They all told her she looked great and that they could see how far she must have come along the road to recovery. Nice folks all.

On the way back from our walk we passed the swimming pool. There we introduced ourselves to Smokie Wolert. He had not met Angela before the crash. He was busy in his volunteer position of keeping an eye on the neighborhood pool and testing and treating the water on a daily basis during the summer. An eighteen-year resident of the neighborhood, he had been disabled for the past fourteen of those years after falling from a tall ladder at work. Smokie offered several valuable insights, likely enhanced by his own disability. He said, "There is a reason for everything and that includes a tragic accident. The challenge is to keep searching for that reason until one discovers it. Once discovered a person can act on it. Do not take your tragedy to your reclining chair and hide from life." Angela thanked him for the advice.

Early on Wednesday we were headed for the Peekskill station to catch a commuter train to Manhattan. Angela had scheduled interviews at Hunter PR. On the way she called out train stops and pointed out landmarks that she thought I would enjoy knowing about. Once we were inside Grand Central Station, Angela insisted upon showing me some of the historic aspects of the station. One of those was the Guastavino tile archway called the Whispering gallery. Here a voice spoken softly into one of the four corners can be clearly heard in the opposing corner perhaps forty feet away even though the station is buzzing with other noise. She giggled as we spoke from corner to corner. My spirits were buoyed with her every laugh, a laugh as genuine as she is. It demonstrates her can-do attitude toward her recovery and toward life in general. If that laugh could be bottled, it could be given as her gift to those who cannot seem to discover their own.

Before crossing the station from the train to the subway, she wanted to swing past one of the gift shops to purchase a fragrance that she had not been able to find since she left the city. She bought a big bottle. A girl just has to have her favorite fragrance.

She was enjoying showing me around, and for my part I felt as though I were being led by a professional tour guide and not by a TBI survivor. She was demonstrating just how well this phase of her long recovery was going. She was remembering the little things about the city she loves.

Angela purchased the subway passes. From Grand Central station it was a two-stop ride downtown on the 6 train to the 28th Street station. From there it was a short walk to the office located on the corner of 26th Street and Madison Avenue. She led the way and walked confidently without stumbling. Once in the lobby, she approached the doorman, Ronnie Rasario. He instantly recognized her and they shared a hug. He told her how much he had missed her and that he had kept up with her progress by talking to Hunter people as they passed through the lobby. Ronnie told us that he could understand what Angela was dealing with because his own son had suffered a serious brain injury. Injured in his early teens, the young man was now married and living a full life. Angela had not known about Ronnie's son. She quickly offered words of encouragement for him to share with his son.

Angela had been telling me for weeks that Hunter PR was a very special company comprised of young public relations professionals with big hearts. In fact, I had heard so much that I had come looking for the heart of Hunter, and I saw it on display that day in interviews and conversations.

In the days, weeks and months that followed that crash, Hunter PR had continued to do for Angela many things they were not contractually obligated to do. Their generous acts were not limited to those required by laws or by heartless "company policy" that some employers limit themselves to following. Their actions were guided by "the heart of Hunter."

In the lobby of Hunter several of her co-workers were ready with a warm welcome. After the greetings, we were taken to a conference room scheduled for our individual and group interviews. As I had done during the interviews at the hospital, I asked Angela to wait outside for portions of some of them. Once past the potential sensitive points of the interview, Angela came back into the room and participated in the dialogue. Those interviewed were completely open and honest.

Interview day at Hunter PR

We talked about many topics: Angela the co-worker, mentor, and great friend in times of personal difficulty for others. We talked too about the day of the crash and the days that followed, very dark days for the Hunter PR team.

Angela's boss, Jon Lyon, provided his perspective about her. Jon had been her boss for her eight years at Hunter. Of Angela, Jon said, "I was her boss but also her friend." Upon hearing him say this, with a smile and a tease she said of Jon, "He was the best boss I ever had. Of course, he was the only boss I ever had." Clearly, these two had coached and counseled each other very effectively over their years together.

Jon said he always looked for the human connection with the people in his life including the Hunter clients. But he said Angela was better at it than he was because she went deeper than he did.

Angela had seen Jon experience some personal losses and had been a source of support for him. Less than a year before Angela's crash, he had lost his mother to Lou Gehrig's disease and then his pet dog of twelve years. He was learning how to deal with loss and grief. Angela's horrific injury was one more struggle for him.

I asked Jon his impressions of her recovery, just thirteen months along. He said, "It's mind-boggling. She looks vibrant. I can see the light in her eyes." He was clearly happy but not surprised. He said, as did others, "Nothing she does really surprises me."

Another significant interview, conducted with Angela out of the room, was with her good friend, Chad Pearson, her co-worker and a close friend at Hunter for six years. He described the first time he saw Angela at Westchester Hospital a couple of days after the crash. She was on one of those automated patient beds that rolled her gently from side to side and moved up and down from end to end. They are designed to help the circulation of a coma patient going while they are confined to that bed. He saw the valve in her skull used to relieve the pressure caused by a swollen brain, the halo surgically screwed into her skull in order to prevent any turning of her head or neck. It was tough for him to see his dear friend that way. It had been tough for all of those who had seen her that way.

Chad said he will never forget the first call he got from Angela after she awoke from the coma and could use the phone in her room. He still keeps it on his answering device. In a thick southern accent that had mysteriously returned to her speech, Angela wished him success in an upcoming Triathlon for which he had been training. He was overwhelmed that in the midst of her suffering, she recalled his event and reached out to wish him well.

As the interview progressed, the special nature of their relationship and some of the reasons for it became clear. A portion of the their relationship was based upon individual losses that they had helped each other to overcome. Chad had suffered after the death of his serious girlfriend, Laura, who had passed away unexpectedly while working in China. Just a year later, Angela had lost her younger sister in a car crash. Now she had lost her husband Rich. There had been intense sadness in both their young lives. I asked Chad his concerns about her future. He offered only one. "I lost a love and she has too. I hope she can find true love again."

Chad said he knew from the moment he heard Angela had survived the crash that she would be okay. He said, "Angela had always lived a purpose driven life." He believed she still would even though that purpose was facing a total make-over.

For lunch, all ordered hamburgers and French fries from the Shake Shack. Someone would have to stand in the long line of customers to pick-up the order. There was always a line at Shake Shack. These hamburgers were something of a tradition periodically renewed at lunchtime by the Hunter team.

The hamburger and fries lunch reminded someone of Angela's generous and somewhat impulsive acts. A couple of years before, she left the office with one of her Hunter friends to get lunch at McDonalds. On the way she saw a homeless person and invited him to come with them. He did and she bought his lunch. At the time, her friend thought it an ill-advised act of kindness. Now, sadly, having suffered a TBI, her future generous acts could make her vulnerable. Impaired judgment could make her actions too bold and expose her to risks. Acts like sincere and compassionate bold hugs given to total strangers could be judged as inappropriate by those around her. Although Angela has never met a stranger, she does have to be more careful now.

During lunch more people dropped in and made caring comments. When one male co-worker entered the room, Angela asked how things were going for him. He reported that his dad had suffered a serious stroke a week earlier but that he was progressing nicely. He said that the medical team had suggested the family should have modest expectations about his recovery. Upon hearing that, Angela went ballistic. She told him that in her own experience with the medical community, the worst-case scenario is always portrayed. She said he should demand that they do everything within their power to get his dad back to full strength again. He should tell them that anything else was just not acceptable. He left the conversation with renewed resolve concerning his father's recovery program. Is it any wonder she was doing so well? All along she had demanded that her doctors and therapists give their best effort. She certainly was giving it her best.

Soon it was time for cup cakes to be served. Having cupcakes together is another tradition at the Hunter office. New Yorkers love their cupcakes as much as we southerners love our biscuits and gravy. The cup cakes served that day were from Grace Leong's favorite baker over in New Jersey. The hearts of Hunter as well as the appetites of Hunter were on display all day long. Great people can make a company a great place to work. Hunter has great people. Is it any wonder that Hunter clients stay with them year after year?

At the time of her crash, Angela had been working on a major client event that was just five days away. Redwood Creek Wines was going to be at a major industry trade show and had expected Angela's help. It was the Outdoor Summer Retailer tradeshow with 4,000 customers and the outdoor press meeting in Salt Lake City. Upon hearing of Angela's tragic crash and life-threatening injuries, editors Jon Dorn and Shannon Davis of Backpacker magazine kept their press colleagues informed.

The event went forward with Gigi and others from Hunter pulling it together. With Angela's famous event planning binder as her guide, Gigi inherited all the important details she needed to carry on. These details included a speech that Angela had written for her client to deliver before a concert given by the well-known band, "Rusted Root." Although the band did not know Angela, they dedicated a song to her. Her client had previously scheduled a hike to the top of a local mountain as one of the concluding highlights of the trade show. They added a spirit-filled vigil at the top of the mountain to focus upon their wishes for her recovery. People were truly moved. Wow!

In the weeks following the crash, several of Angela's clients demonstrated their thoughtfulness by sending gifts, cards, and personal messages that indicated their affection for her and for Hunter. It is hard to imagine just how high her spirits were lifted by the expressions of love and support from her clients. Clients and many others followed her progress on her Caring Bridge account.

Grace Leong joined our group interview. She is President of the firm and the boss of those we were meeting with that day. An incredibly busy person, she took a major slice out of her day to be involved and to share her own Angela stories and wisdom. One of those stories was that Angela's husband Rich had so often sent flowers to the office. It put real pressure on the men at Hunter to be more romantic with the women in their lives. The women of Hunter were simply envious of Angela.

Grace also recalled that a week before the crash, Angela had asked people to come out to a concert Rich and his band had scheduled. Rich was a talented but yet to be discovered musician. Angela was his loving and supportive wife. That was the "concert" that went ahead as scheduled with Rich's band playing no music; their grief was heavy.

With some of what Grace and others were reporting, Angela responded that she could not remember the memory they were sharing with her. Grace shared a lesson she learned in childhood when Grace complained to her mother that she could not remember something, her mother had said, "Grace, things you have experienced are in your memory but you may not be able to recall them all." Grace recommended that Angela start using the expression, "I cannot recall." Angela found the suggestion helpful and made the subtle but positive change.

Grace had additional deep thoughts that afternoon. She said, "We all knew Angela would come out of her injuries and make a great life." She felt, "God selected Angela because He knew that she would turn her personal loss into a gift for others."

As our time together went along that day, Hunter people became more comfortable with sharing what was deepest in their hearts.

Dear friend Gigi answered my question about how people there felt after the news of the crash had settled in on them. She summed it up for herself, and likely for others, by saying she had been very angry at first. How could something like this happen to someone as wonderful as her friend Angela? Next her emotions changed to sadness for Angela and for the families of both Rich and Angela. She wished for her a debt free if not a wealthy life. Angela deserved a future with far fewer troubles. Her final wish was that Angela have a love-filled life.

When I asked if Angela's tragedy had changed the lives of her friends at Hunter, again Gigi offered the most candid and profound comment. She had seen Angela move fearlessly through her loss and into recovery. Gigi was married and now pregnant for the first time. She said, in the presence of her co-workers, "After seeing how fearlessly Angela handled life and now aware that I too could suddenly lose my own husband, I had the courage I needed to give new life." The room fell silent. They understood what Gigi meant as each of them had been changed in intensely personal ways. All seemed intent on living life more fearlessly.

Since Angela's tragic crash, the people of Hunter experienced positive changes in the workplace. There seemed to be more kindness and thoughtfulness in the air. These employees had always thought Hunter was a great place to work. Seeing how the management and the team had come together in response to Angela's situation, they were now certain that it was.

Angela had been very much in love with Rich. She had recently written a letter to him she planned to leave on his grave during our planned visit there on Friday. She read the letter to her Hunter friends. The room grew very quiet. People were moved by and even beyond the words she was reading.

Before we left Hunter that day, Angela expressed her intention to have a memorial** service for Rich. She wanted them to come but that she needed more time to heal before scheduling it. Of course, that included the need for emotional healing.

*** The memorial celebration of Rich's life occurred a year later in August, 2010, at the Explorer's Club. My wife and I attended and listened as friends of both Rich and Angela took turns sharing thoughts about how both had impacted their lives. The comments about Rich were wide-ranging. He was described as compassionate, sensitive, responsive, talented, funny, professional, dedicated, persistent and thorough. Although we had never met him, the comments that night had us wishing that we had. Angela had chosen well.*

We said good-bye and left Hunter's offices in time for Angela to take a late nap at the nearby apartment of friend Jennifer. I had a beer in a local pub and waited for her to get ready for an important dinner reunion at her favorite restaurant, Blue Smoke and Jazz Standard, on East 27th near Lexington Avenue.

The folks at Blue Smoke made this evening special as they had so many times over the years for Angela and her friends. Wine and spirits director, Tinika Green, and *chef de cuisine*, Jason Krantz, came by our table to visit briefly with Angela. Their warmth was real. They had heard she was doing well and were visibly relieved to see the living proof of it.

This evening's specialness was not the first time Blue Smoke showed concern for Angela. After Angela had relocated to North Carolina, Mair contacted Angela's friend and noted food/ entertainment reviewer, Joanna Priscoe, to update her on the recovery. Joanna knew Angela was fond of Blue Smoke food, fond being an understatement. Without telling anyone about her plan, Joanna contacted Blue Smoke. Upon hearing about Angela's situation, they sent Angela a Blue Smoke sampler to North Carolina by over-night package delivery. They included a note that they had been told she wanted her first meal outside the hospital to be from Blue Smoke; they sent her that meal. Her spirits were lifted when a little slice of home came her way.

That evening, as we were leaving, Angela gave the Blue Smoke team the big thanks they were due. They informed us that our wonderful meal for our party of five was provided with their compliments.

Our dinner guest that evening was Ken (K. J.) Reardon, one of the paramedics on the helicopter the night of the crash. For Angela and K. J. this was an emotional meeting. However, the emotions were those of joy.

K. J. told us something of his background. He had started his work life in the employ of a large corporation, but he hated what he was expected to do there. He left and trained as an EMT. Desiring more professional challenge, he took more training and became a paramedic. In all his eighteen years as a paramedic, many of those on an evacuation helicopter, this was the first time he had ever met with one of its surviving passengers.

After the crash he had stopped in at Westchester once while Angela was in her coma. He told us that he rarely checks to see how his trauma patients are doing. He said all too many that are involved in crashes like that one simply do not make it. In many ways he and the flight crew were surprised that Angela had.

After that evening at Blue Smoke with K. J., we conducted phone interviews with the lead paramedic, Rob Kallen, and nurse, Janna Canavan, from that life flight helicopter crew. They gave us a clear picture of the role they play.

Extensive and ongoing training is required of all life flight crew members. Rob indicated that they are careful not to go beyond those procedures in which they have been adequately trained. Every one of their cases are later reviewed by a medical director. Yet, with all of their training and the care given under the most demanding of conditions, the flight crew is sometimes the target of lawsuits by patients and their families claiming mistakes were made or that there was malpractice. I had mistakenly assumed that because the flight crew required extensive training, dealing with challenging medical emergencies, working 24 hour shifts and flying into difficult and dangerous landing sites, they were likely paid an extremely high wage—a false assumption. Many who serve in this high stress role must have second jobs to pay their living expenses.

Why would anyone aspire to serve on a life flight helicopter? What attracts top medical talent to do it? Janna put it this way: "We see all kinds of cases and have an opportunity to broaden our skills. For a nurse, it is the ultimate challenge."

Paramedic Rob Kallen said he is not out there "saving lives." Instead he believes that he is "involved with preventing deaths." Unless one thinks about this comment it appears to be a distinction without a difference. Given some thought it becomes clear that saving lives requires omniscience while preventing death (at least for a time until others can take charge of the patient) requires only the use of his training and the application of his skills.

Rob again reiterated that the entire crew was surprised that Angela had survived that night and the early days following the crash. There is no way to thank them sufficiently for what they did for her.

Over and over again, all that week, my unfounded bias about New Yorkers being superficial and selfish was repeatedly challenged by their actual behavior. I had only infrequently visited in the past. Many conventional beliefs about New Yorkers come from people like me who have never lived there or gotten to know the people of the city. Good people can be found everywhere if we are open to the possibility.

It was a short cab ride to Grand Central station for the 9 PM train back to Peekskill station and the short car ride back to Putnam Valley and the Floridan neighborhood. Angela had done very well on this very long day that was demanding both physically and emotionally.

Thursday we faced the issues surrounding her home. I told Angela that I had over forty years of home owning experience. My wife and I had moved with our children on five separate occasions. If I could use that experience to her benefit I would be happy to do it. She asked me to participate fully in all the tasks and meetings that day.

We met with her real estate sales people. The home had been on the market for several months, with essentially no buyer interest shown in it. It was a nice home, fairly priced but offered in a dead real estate market.

This was the first home she had ever purchased; nothing too fancy but a great starter home for the young couple. Now it had to be disposed of as expeditiously as possible. Her double vision persisted and she could not drive. She was not ready to live independently so far from the city and all the therapists who still needed to work with her.

There were discussions of a "short sale" and Angela gave the real estate people the go ahead to pursue it. She would not be able to live there again and mortgage payments and upkeep were much too much for her to manage now.

Wishing to notify the mortgage holding bank of her brain injury and cash flow dilemma, Angela decided to write a "hardship letter." She hoped to gain a reasonable revision in her payment terms. She wrote that hardship letter herself. When I read it before she sent it, her words seemed to understate her hardship. In no way was she playing the sympathy card. She handled this as a matter of personal business that needed attention.

Before sending the letter, Angela had her childhood friend Neysa Borkert, a successful attorney in Florida, look it over. Neysa also reviewed the short sell agreement with the realtors. It was difficult for Neysa to see Angela in the position of considering both the short sell and simultaneously asking a big bank to consider revised her mortgage payment terms. No short sell offer came from any buyer. The letter explaining her difficult circumstances did not move the bank as it never responded to the letter.

Thank goodness for Neysa. Angela could not afford an attorney to look over every important issue confronting her. When Neysa finally convinced Angela to allow her to help pro bono, valuable time had been lost and dollars had already been spent. Angela had been far too sensitive about asking for or even allowing people to help.

Legal service is one of many things many brain injured people must acquire. In fact, Neysa strongly suggested that every young person, upon reaching the age of majority, prepare legal documents that may be needed to cover their own medical emergencies and death. For example, when she was already in a coma it was too late for Angela to decide on a medical power of attorney. That document would have prevented confusion and disagreement between her parents following the crash that injured Angela.

We had a few hours left that day to work our way down the list of things that needed to be done at her home. She was concerned about some badly worn and missing shingles on a couple of sections of the roof. She did not want her renters to have leaks to deal with in the second floor apartment. At the neighborhood community center I inquired about the availability of a good handyman. It happened that one of the neighbors hanging out there at that time did that type of work; he came right over. He offered to do the job for a fair price. Angela told him to go ahead and the repairs were completed a few days after we left.

Angela had to decide what to do with the furnishings of her home. She knew that if and when she moved back to a small apartment in the city the furniture would not fit. We marked a few select pieces of furniture with blue masking tape to designate the items she wanted to keep. The moving company would know, by the blue tape designation, which pieces she wanted to have stored and which were to be disposed of. We had a moving and storage company come to provide an estimate. Another task accomplished in our busy week.

Before we left, there was also some cleaning to do. A home gets dusty even when nobody lives in it. We dusted and put some cushions out in the sun to freshen them. We cleaned the bathroom fixtures and the kitchen surfaces. It looked neat and orderly.

She had new renters in the second floor apartment. She met them and was satisfied that this young couple would take care of the place and pay the rent on time. This was their first home. They had already been keeping the grass cut and the weeds down. They were doing thoughtful chores for a landlady to whom they owed nothing but their rent money. They were special young people.

Neighbors came to say a final good bye. At last, near the end of another busy day, Angela packed some clothing she would need for the approaching winter in North Carolina. We would be leaving in the morning.

This is as good a time as any to share the financial reality that hit Angela as it does so many brain injured people. With a sustained and perhaps permanent loss of income and huge bills, many TBI survivors quickly begin to resemble a financial train-wreck. She certainly did.

Her personal finances were a sensitive subject to introduce into our relationship. I wasn't sure that her precarious financial situation was any of my business. After all, my job was originally defined as one of writing a book about her recovery from the brain injury. Yet her financial situation was serious and she had to deal with it daily. How could I write an honest account of her recovery without including some financial information? How could I respect her privacy while becoming a more concerned friend with each passing day? I decided to approach this subject and if she told me to back off I would. She did not do that. She needed someone older she could trust, someone who did not have a personal stake in her financial future.

What I learned was not good news. Here, without allowing her to share with me the specific balance from her bank account or her credit card balances, was what she faced.

When Rich died in the crash his income stopped. As a responsible young couple, they had been actively pursuing but had not yet acquired an insurance policy on his life. She had no life insurance money to help her along.

Her divorced parents wanted to help and did what they could. However, neither was financially able to do much. Angela's income had stopped too. Hunter Public Relations did all they could through their employee medical benefits plan. They went well beyond what a less sensitive company would have done. However, when medical benefits stopped, Angela was on her own. She had nothing coming in and a steady and growing stream of expenses.

It was obvious that her home had to be disposed of soon in one way or another. There was a huge inventory of homes for sale in the area so a fast sale at a fair price seemed remote. She would likely lose the home to foreclosure and with that her credit rating would take a heavy hit.

She had to pay for her monthly mortgage, rent, food, expensive medications, doctors and therapy services, and her adopted dog's frequent vet bills. She cut as many expenses as she could. Yet all her expenses had to be paid for from her disability check. Impossible.

Attorney Marc Rich filed a lawsuit in Angela's behalf not long after the crash. He vigorously pursued the settlement because he knew Angela was in tough financial shape. Resolution of lawsuits can take years and the outcome is always in doubt. She was falling deeper into debt every day. Something had to give; perhaps it would be the defendants.

The investigation and reconstruction of the crash made several facts very clear. The driver of the tractor trailer was speeding. Written records admitted into evidence by the judge showed that the driver had left the terminal quite late and seemed intent on making up the time he had lost. The equipment he was driving had a questionable maintenance history. In fact, the trailer had been wrecked and heavily damaged once before. After a crash involving a fatality, that trailer should have been impounded. But in direct violation of the law, the owner had it scrapped and the evidence it held was destroyed. Damages seemed clearly due her.

Two years later, Angela is still waiting and a possible settlement date is not in sight. Will she get any settlement and will it be enough to pay for her modest lifestyle needs for at least a few years? She is now thirty-two years old and unlikely to ever again work for a significant wage because of her loss of cognitive skills.

What settlement amount might restore her to financial health? How about an eventual settlement of one or two million dollars? That sounds like a lot of money, but not so. From any settlement she may receive, the dollars would first be distributed to pay her attorney, settle any liens attached to the settlement by her bank and hospitals, pay down her credit card and catch up on other bills. Her medical bills alone exceed $800,000 and continue to grow.

Those settlement dollars would dwindle very quickly. Angela understands that her financial future does not look bright, and yet she is able to flash her "oh well" smile of acceptance.

A brain injury survivor faces additional personal business complexities. All at once after the injury, close attention must be paid to insurance policies and claims, living expenses from housing to utilities, investments, taxes, cash management, pet care, auto payments and licenses. The list is even longer if the TBI survivor owns a small business or is self employed. All these items may not become issues for all survivors and their loved ones but some are sure to be.

The brain injury recovery issues alone are more than enough for a TBI patient to have to manage. Qualified help will be needed from people who can be trusted. Just who can be trusted with decisions and distributions of such magnitude? Where money is involved, care must be taken.

The added burden of so many complex and urgent personal business issues piled on top of the recovery issues seems unfair. Of course, nothing is fair about a traumatic brain injury.

On Friday morning we took one last look around, locked the door and backed out of the driveway. It was apparent that she was leaving her home for good. She took one long last look but did not comment or cry. While some doors were closing, she felt sure that eventually some new doors were going to open for her.

We were headed for her first visit with Rich's parents since the weeks immediately following the crash. Angela had not seen them since leaving for North Carolina. The Betancourts were awaiting us at their Tenafly, NJ, home. She greeted them by affectionately calling them "Mom and Dad." She had done that since she and Rich were married and she saw no reason to stop now. We also spent some time with his only sibling, sister Denise.

As hugs were shared, tears were too, the type of tears that come with being over-whelmed with the meaning of life. Those tears were easy to understand but were quickly replaced by conversation. None of them wanted to spend this short time together consumed by tears. The Betancourts wanted to know how she was doing. She was equally interested in finding out how they were doing.

Angela reminded mom Betancourt of the gift she had given to Angela. When she and Rich had visited,

Angela had admired, even coveted, a pair of red high-heeled shoes her mother-in-law was wearing. While she was still in the hospital, those red high heels were gift-wrapped and presented to Angela. With her brain still not functioning all that well, Angela recognized the shoes and Mom Betancourt's thoughtfulness in giving them to her. She fully intended to go dancing in them one day. Mom Betancourt was delighted to hear her say that.

Angela told us that while she was in rehabilitation in North Carolina she had shown up for a physical therapy session on the treadmill wearing a pair of high heels. This is not conventional footwear for use on a treadmill, even one with a weightless harness. But then little about Angela that is conventional. She admitted that her legs were cramped for two days after that session. It had been worth it to her.

Before lunch, Mom drove us to the cemetery to visit Rich's grave. It was Angela's first visit there. She was in a coma when his funeral was held two days after the crash. She and her mother-in-law walked to the grave arm-in-arm. I stood behind them choking back my tears. Their sadness did not last too long as their happy shared memories about Rich soon brought smiles to their faces. Angela wrote a beautiful love letter and left it on his grave. She allowed both of us to read it. Here is what she wrote:

Dear Rich,

Hello my love. I can feel you watching this pen touch the page but I'll leave this letter at your grave for you to reread anytime you'd like. I hope to find pieces of your memory on this trip to New York but admit that I'm scared of the emotions that may come too.

Thank you for being such an incredible guardian angel and allowing me to feel your presence every day. It must be hard work! You keep very busy! Isn't my handwriting looking great?! Not quite the penmanship found in my old love letters to you, but not bad for having to relearn how to write.

I know that this is where you lay to rest but that is all. The hollow shell of your body can't possibly house your enormous spirit that touches people across the world every day. I hope to honor your spirit in the book I'm working on that will capture our story and honor the team of strangers who came together to save my life.

Will you help me find a path to pay this blessing forward? I want to share your love for me by helping others who are experiencing this challenge, families and their loved one who have TBIs. But I don't know how to just yet. If you're guiding me, I know I'll figure it out.

I love you as much today as the day we first met. The day we got married. The day we bought our first home. Moses misses his Daddy. I miss you too, but at least you left your voice behind for the world to enjoy whenever we need you.

Goodbye my love,
Angela

Angela leaves her letter to Rich

Before leaving the cemetery, we visited the beautiful chapel where Rich's funeral services took place. We went back to the Betancourt home to share a nice lunch they had prepared. All said their good-byes and we headed back to North Carolina. After several hours of driving and as darkness approached, we checked into a northern Virginia motel for some much needed rest. Our long return drive was completed late the next afternoon. The drive gave us plenty of time to talk about the trip and about life.

Through the week on the road, Angela relied on her iPhone alarm to remind her to take her meds after breakfast and dinner. She used the full features of the iPhone without confusion, something I likely could not have done. Her stamina was still quite low so she needed a nap sometime every afternoon. I saw that she ate three good meals a day. Already aware of the health implications of her diet, she knew of her "need to have a salad and some veggies."

We had anticipated that this would be a very busy week and it had been. Fatigue, both physical and emotional, could have overtaken her (or me for that matter) but they did not. I was prepared to deal with issues a TBI survivor might experience at this stage of recovery. None of them happened nor showed any sign that they were about to happen. She was physically strong and walked without stumbles or hesitation. At no point did she get frustrated, maudlin, fretful, or say or do anything inappropriate with anyone we met. She laughed easily and enjoyed the memories, even those that had a more bitter than sweet quality. She denied nothing that had happened, and her expectations about her future were appropriately moderated by uncertainty.

I developed one concern during that week. Angela could not seem to thank people enough for the kindness they had shown her since the crash. She would thank them, give them a hug when leaving, and turn again to them to call out one more thank you. Then after we had left them she would say that she needed to get them something to make sure they knew how much she appreciated what they had done. Her need to thank people seemed to be excessive. She had no reason to feel deficient in her expressions of appreciation. In her situation, feeling indebted to people would be natural and is easy to understand. However, tracking individuals down, looking them in the eyes and opening her heart with the specifics of how they had helped her should have been enough. It simply was not enough for her. Not yet anyway.

I gathered my courage, collected my thoughts and then came right out and told her that she needed to let go of this constant sense of obligation. People had done what they had done and she had abundantly and individually thanked them. It was time to move on. She listened and reflected on my comments. Over the next few days she assured me that she understood and agreed with my assessment. The burden of never-ending "thank you" seemed to leave her.

Angela is also a hugger; she always has been. When she sees someone she knows her natural instinct is to give them a big hug. She does it to demonstrate how happy she is to see them again. It was interesting to stand back and watch the varied reactions of those she was hugging. Some jumped right in and warmly hugged her. Others were awkward in the moment and returned her hug in a mechanical manner that suggested returning her hug was an obligation. Being a hugger myself, I felt sorry for those who missed a significant opportunity.

Angela was already planning to move back to Manhattan, unafraid to do so "at an appropriate time in the future when I will not burden the people around me there." Seeing her operate on this trip left me confident that in time she would return. Like others who know and love her, we all felt confident in her getting back home.

She kept reminding us that she is "a big city girl and a New Yorker at heart." It was impossible not to believe in her resolve. In fact, that resolve was a crucial force in her recovery. Life lived without challenging goals does not benefit a TBI survivor or anyone really.

There were compelling reasons for making this trip. It was certainly a trip to see and thank the people who had been so important to her both before and after the crash. It also allowed her to conduct important personal business. But a third reason for making the trip had been less obvious to both of us and we had not talked about it at all. Like the third rail on the subway, this third reason is where all the electricity is found. This was her time for saying good-bye to her first life.

It was one good-bye after another. Good-bye to her therapists at Helen Hayes, her position at Hunter PR, her home and neighbors in the Floridan neighborhood. If not good-bye, it was at least so-long to her old friends and to the Betancourt family. They would still care about her and want to stay in touch. But in the future they would be experiencing a different person.

For me, our NYC trip was an intense immersion into the life of a young woman who, in one week of travel together, became as dear to me as she is to so many who know her. As we returned to North Carolina and up the last mountain to her father's home, I was certain that this book would be written and that the end of it would be report on a positive recovery outcome and renewed hope for her future.

Upon our return I had to complete one important piece of business: write a trip report. I felt it might be helpful to her support team, her family, therapists, physicians and psychologists to read an honest accounting of what had happened and how she handled it. I had observed every aspect of how she dealt with people and events. The distributed report did not exaggerate or edit anything out. To have done that would not be helpful to her support team. Those who received the report thanked me for writing it. Her dad Charlie was especially reassured by its contents and appreciative of my efforts.

Angela Leigh Tucker as told by Bill Ramsey

9

Wrapping up Recovery

After our return from New York I sensed that Angela's confidence had begun to soar. She now knew with near certainty that she was returning to live in Manhattan. All that remained for her to complete the North Carolina phase of recovery were some therapy sessions and preparing her family to accept her decision.

She reflected on the trip. What had she learned about herself and her new reality? A few days later, Angela made another tough decision; tough decisions were necessary in her new life. This one was especially so. She knew she had to tender her resignation from Hunter PR.

She had loved her work there. It was what she had been born to do. As much as the work, she loved those she had worked with for eight years. Grace, Jon, Gigi, Chad, Christine, Michael and so many others were like family to her. Her clients had become her friends too. She understood that those friends would not ever completely forget her; she would certainly not forget them. She also understood that she did not have the cognitive skills, vision, and stamina required to continue as a contributor there. Failing to remember a key task or deadline, not being able to read extensively and needing a nap every afternoon meant she could not expect to keep up the pace required in her past position.

Her letter of resignation was brief, each word carefully considered. She wanted Hunter management to know how much she appreciated and loved them. She wanted them to know how hard it was for her to write this letter without making it difficult for them to read it – emotionally difficult.

She told me the letter was ready to be sent. I realized how tough it must be for Angela to end such an important relationship when so many other vital relationships had already abruptly ended or were greatly diminished. For each of us, those we love function as our life support. Without knowing exactly where her new life support would come from, Angela was pulling the plug. She would leave Hunter PR but her impact on the company and its people would last for many more years.

It was time for her to get back to the work of rehabilitation. She had to become stronger if she was to move back to New York City. Her physical therapy continued at the Reuter Family YMCA located in Biltmore Park, in the same building as the CarePartners offices that Angela visited for other services.

The Executive Director of this YMCA branch, Mary Michael, was another of those who extended an unexpected kindness to Angela and her family. Dad Charlie drove Angela to these physical therapy sessions and waited in the reception area each time until Angela was finished. Seeing a man she had not met sitting there day after day made Mary curious enough to ask him who he was and why he was there so often. When Charlie told her of Angela and his support of her recovery program, Mary immediately offered him complimentary use of their facility so that he could constructively fill his time. She didn't have to do that. She saw a young woman and a family in need and did the right thing. Charlie had certainly earned the kindness she extended.

Incidentally, this YMCA was fully equipped with "intelligent" computer-managed exercise machines. These machines tracked the exercise settings and recorded the time and the repetitions during a workout. Cardio equipment recorded the pulse rate. The physical therapy client or anyone else using the equipment simply typed in his user number and the equipment set itself for that user's prescribed exercise program. After the session, a patient and therapy team could look at those results and adjust the program as needed. Equipment used by brain injury patients has come a long way in the past ten years. With simpler equipment the brain injured person could exceed sensible limits without being aware of it. When cognition is limited, the availability of "smart" equipment is a plus. An unattended visit to a more traditionally equipped gym could be dangerous to a patient with stamina and balance problems.

From the day she arrived in North Carolina, Angela had an ongoing need for as much physical therapy as she could schedule. Mary Wall knew the professionals at Pisgah Physical Therapy and Sports Rehab. She explained to owners Gary and Linda Thiry that Angela's cash and insurance coverage were both exhausted. They offered to provide their service at no charge. Imagine the value of that kind offer. Gary and his assistant Kristin Neuburger gave her the sessions she so desperately needed. While in their care, she benefitted from using an advanced type of treadmill not commonly found in therapy practices. A "weightless" treadmill allowed Angela to relearn the movements needed to walk but removed the stress and risk of supporting the weight of her own body. After successfully walking weightlessly, she was better prepared to walk as one normally would on a standard treadmill.

Another was a developmental psychologist, Trisha Miller, PhD, a clinical psychologist. Much of her practice was with young children and teens but the needs of adults are frequently served by developmental psychologists. She described the needs of brain injured adult clients as "re-developmental."

High heels on a treadmill?

183

Trisha needed a starting point with Angela and getting to know her was the first step. She asked Charlie to come to a couple of sessions. Angela needed his help in recalling some things that had happened in her childhood.

Hearing these childhood highlights helped Trisha know what to expect from the patient. She described it as a "connect the dots" kind of exercise.

The second step involved reading the daily journals Angela had kept and willingly shared with Trisha. Reading the highlights from them was very helpful in defining the course the therapy should take. Her patient's thoughts and concerns were clearer when stated in the client's own written words. The journals were yet another useful tool that Angela had created.

Trisha interviewed and observed Angela and discovered that she had temporarily lost some important social skills. For example, she would enter a room full of people and plunge right into conversations. Angela needed to reacquire her ability to enter a room and observe what was going on before getting involved.

Another of Angela's impulses was to anticipate the direction a question or conversation was taking and jump in with a response that was off the mark and not fitting. Her answer often missed the question the other person was attempting to ask. She could be interpreted as rude or a poor listener when neither of those two things was even close to being true of her. She simply needed to listen longer and control her impulses better.

In their sessions together, once Angela agreed with Trisha's assessment target they went to work on it together. Absent a patient's agreement it is futile for the therapist to push a solution unless and until the patient accepts the assessment of an observed need.

Trisha also pointed out that when a patient is in a highly emotional state, that emotion must first be dealt with or the therapy will not work. She explained that emotion over-rides cognition in brain injured clients. Trisha used the first few minutes of each session to assess the emotional state Angela might be in that day.

Angela was still taking small doses of Lexapro and Depakote to stabilize her wake/sleep cycles and level her moods a little. Trisha suggested to Angela that when the time was right for putting them aside it would happen. For now, however, these drugs were allowing them to do the work that needed to be done. Neither of them wanted to lose valuable rehabilitation time to problems that a low dose of these drugs could help her to avoid. Angela was eager to stop the drugs, but for now at least, taking them was better than not taking them would have been.

Angela shared one incident that had occurred since her return to live with Charlie. One morning she reported to her dad that she did not feel at all like herself that morning. When they checked her medication dispenser they discovered that Angela had not taken her medicine for three days. With that discovery she went right back on the medications and returned to feeling and acting like herself. After that experience, she tried to use reminders on to-do lists she wrote for herself. That did not work because she did not always remember to read those lists. When she used her iPhone with all its programmable audible alarms and reminders, much of her forgetting began to matter less. When she traveled or was back in NYC that phone would prove to be a great help.

Prior to suffering her TBI, Angela had lived independently without the need for help from others to accomplish everyday, ordinary things. The TBI changed that. She now needed help. While always appreciative when someone volunteered, Angela found it hard to ask anyone. Trisha convinced Angela that many people were ready and willing to help her. Her requests would be welcomed more often than she might believe.

For example, Angela had wanted to go to church on Sundays. She had no ride and was reluctant to ask anyone from her church to provide her with one. When she finally asked, a neighbor woman, Geri Conley, stepped forward to provide the needed rides. She was happy to do it. All Angela had needed to do was ask.

She signed up for one more therapy, one that many brain injured people may not know about or try. It is reflexology. Regarded by some as a controversial healing art, reflexology uses pressure applied specific zones of the feet and hands to effect physical changes in the body. Into her rehabilitation regime came reflexology therapist David Henry to help her with her balance problems. Angela was interested in trying non-traditional approaches along with mainline therapies. Why not? She believes there is much to be said for the healing power of human touch.

When David first began working with Angela he had to assist her down the hallway and onto the treatment table in his office. It was difficult for her to remove her shoes so he helped.

When he soon identified additional benefits that he believed would accrue to her from the application of facial reflexology, he rushed to gain certification training in this very specific area of reflexology. The help he provided included giving her ways to think about her double vision. He could not eliminate it, but could provide her with some exercises and demonstrate how to turn her head in the direction of what she needed to see. That worked better at easing the double vision than simply moving her eyes up and down and from side to side.

Many months later Angela found a renowned neuro-optomitrist in NYC who prescribed special lenses for her glasses. They greatly reduced the problem. After getting them she asked me to try them on. Those glasses actually reversed my normal and clear vision making me see double. I saw what she had been seeing, actually not seeing, for almost two years. Everything was immediately and completely unfocused. I was made dizzy in a few seconds. Yet she had managed without those special lenses by frequently wearing an eye-patch.

My interviews with therapists and physicians were intended to help me understand brain injuries in general and Angela's brain injury in particular. They were all helpful and shared one thing in common in the interviews and in their work. Without using patient names, they talked about what their patients had needed in brain injury therapy. They were comparing Angela's needs to the needs of their past patients; those patients whose needs most closely matched hers. Very rarely did they refer to any learned papers or studies that had been conducted on brain injured people. When they did it was only by way of explaining their profession to me. They never indicated that some article in a professional journal had given them the information they needed to deal effectively with Angela. It was obvious that they were learning from each and every patient. I came to understand clearly what is meant by the term "in my therapy practice."

When questioned about their early days just after they had finished formal training, some therapists acknowledged being " scared to death that I would say the wrong thing to a client." After a few years they realized that if they did say something unhelpful, the patient would provide the feedback required for them to work through the issue and resume effective therapy. That discovery made them more self-assured in their practice.

In Angela's experience there was only one irreparable comment made by one of her therapists. Angela came to her session eager to report on what she regarded as a major breakthrough in her recovery and the insight it had given her. She shared it with the therapist and got a hurtful response: "Well, Angela, anyone could have done that." She was shocked at the thoughtless response. The comment completely discounted what Angela had done and was obviously unprofessional. She soon broke her ties with that therapist after first telling her why she was leaving the practice. She did what all brain injury survivors need to do. She asked questions of her therapists and stood up for herself. As this atypical and insensitive therapist clearly demonstrated, TBI survivors are not the only people with lessons to learn.

Each of her therapists said that as they gained experience they felt more confident with each patient they handled. Angela did not work with any single therapist for very long, yet based upon their years of experience, her therapists really seemed to know her. At least what they knew of her matched very nicely with what her other therapists had come to know of her. My observations, although those of a non-therapist, were consistent with what they were telling me about her. It was very reassuring and suggested that my friend had indeed been treated as an individual. They had tailored their therapy to meet her individual and specific needs. Her recovery has been greatly enhanced by their care.

When a patient makes progress there is a point at which both the patient and the therapist seem to agree that their sessions together need to end. When the patient comes in and does not have much to talk about, the session takes on a chatty tone. "What did you do this weekend? Did you see a good movie?" Some chatty patients may be reluctant to cut the cord as they have come to regard the therapist as their friend. Sometimes that therapist may be the only person who is really listening to the patient. However, a therapy professional never crosses the line to allow the patient to become a friend in the usual sense of that word. They do not go out together socially. The therapist does not share personal problems with the patient.

Angela was very good at knowing herself and what was working for her. Several times over the two years of her recovery she would tell the therapist that they needed to reduce the time spent in scheduled sessions or even cancel future sessions. She was always very polite and never acted out of anger or frustration with the therapist. The guidance she provided regarding her own recovery was helpful to all.

Her self-awareness was acute. She knew her brain injury related problems. Given enough time, she knew that her team of practicing professionals could deduce them. If she knew she needed help with a specific problem, Angela did not wait for them to figure it out. She let them know so they could more effectively work together.

One of those problems was her co-dependency. Angela was aware that she had suffered with a co-dependence tendency before the TBI. This was especially true in her relationships with her parents. She wanted that relationship to be more adult to adult. She certainly loved and needed them but she felt herself always trying to please them and putting their needs ahead of her own. Interested in knowing more about co-dependency, Angela read a book on the subject. Her double vision slowed her reading rate and was tiring but she did finish the book. Once she had read the way co-dependency manifests itself, she had the confirmation she needed to seek help from her psychologist. Self-help was a strong supplement to the help from her professional team. Often in her recovery, she identified a possible problem before her professional resources had time to see it. She did nothing to deny her issues and never hid them from those that could provide her with insight about them.

Therapists and psychologists were always most complimentary of Angela saying they saw in her a person who was wise beyond her years. She was even more wise than many people her age who had never suffered a severe brain injury. Angela responded that at times she felt like she had the wisdom of her own grandmother wrapped up in the body of a thirty year-old. She doesn't focus upon and dither about the small and unimportant things in her life as some of her young friends seem to do. She does not claim to be better than they are, just a little more aware of those things in life that truly matter.

Of course, her days were filled with more than therapy sessions. Angela was learning all she could about traumatic brain injuries and developing her advocacy skills. The more she did the more she found she could do. It was as though she was successfully climbing an invisible ladder.

In North Carolina, she attended the monthly meetings of a brain injury support group called "Meeting of the Minds." This program is a part of the out-reach of the Brain Injury Association of North Carolina. Karen Harrington, the Community Outreach Coordinator and the facilitator for these meetings, is a dedicated and sensitive person. Angela really liked her.

At first, Angela attended simply as a person who had suffered a brain injury months earlier. However, not long after joining the group, she discovered that her role was evolving. She had been in her own recovery stage for less than a year but had made some progress. Her progress positioned her to provide help to those who had more recently suffered a TBI and others who seemed to be stuck in one place in their recovery. Karen saw what was happening and encouraged Angela to keep giving her gift to others. She enabled Angela to do all she had the time and energy to do. Karen knew what she was doing. Her feedback encouraged Angela to recognize and acknowledge her recovery progress and to dig still deeper for more. By giving help to others, Angela was learning more about herself and gaining confidence about her future.

Both Karen and Sandra Farmer, Executive Director of the Brain Injury Association of North Carolina, saw Angela's interest and capability. They decided to include her in a March 12, 2009, trip to Washington, DC, to help them educate some congressional leaders about traumatic brain injury and the needs of survivors at the National Traumatic Brain Injury Awareness Day. The small delegation from North Carolina met and spoke with our senators and our district congressional representative. Angela was not bashful in her comments. After all, an effective advocate cannot be bashful and mute.

The Association had also scheduled a fund raising event called "Joggin' for the Noggin" for late in March.

The brain injured members of the group were not going to run or even walk in the event. Their task was to seek event participants and donor sponsors. Angela found donors, more donors than anyone else. In doing so she won the top prize—airfare and a one-week stay in a timeshare apartment in Las Vegas. Use of the timeshare had been contributed to the Association. She was thrilled to accept the award. Even with all her prior business travel, she had never been to Las Vegas.

Not yet able to travel alone, she asked a couple of friends to go along. Gigi Russo from Hunter PR and Monica Sety, her occupational therapist from CarePartners, were both thrilled to go. Her family had strongly suggested that a therapist go along. In late September, 2009, she was on the plane for Las Vegas.

Consistent with her lifelong approach to opportunities like those presented by this trip, Angela scheduled a variety of activities. She took a helicopter ride with Monica over the Grand Canyon and the Hoover Dam. Gigi obtained tickets to the Cirque Du Soleil show. All three went to the spa for the works, very lightly hit the game tables, sat by the pool and visited. In a concession to her low energy level, all agreed to have Angela grab some naps and to get her to bed at night by nine.

Her commitment to advocacy kept growing. She planned to attend the annual state meeting co-sponsored by the North Carolina Brain Injury Association and Wake AHEC. This one-day meeting of professionals, attended by a sprinkling of brain injured people, is held each fall in the state capital of Raleigh. She wanted me to take her there and I jumped at the opportunity. I still had a lot to learn.

At the opening reception on Thursday evening, there was time to meet people and to see some of our North Carolina legislators get recognition for their support of brain injury research and treatment.

The Friday schedule was packed with informative and inspiring presentations by brain injury survivors, doctors and researchers. Exhibitors were in the hall during the day. Some attendees earned licensing-related CEU credits for participating.

The highlight of the evening program came when Lee Woodruff stepped up to the microphone and told the story of her husband Bob Woodruff. Her presentation covered some of the highlights from her book, *In An Instant*. Bob Woodruff is a handsome and talented television news journalist for the ABC television network. After years of broadcasting accomplishment, he was promoted to the evening news anchor position. The war in Iraq was being fiercely contested and Bob wanted to report from the front. As he was observing the fight, he momentarily raised his head above the tank he was riding in. At that precise moment, an insurgent bomb went off and he suffered a severe brain injury.

With complete honesty, Lee told about the impact of that injury on Bob, herself and their young children. As bad as his injury had been, and it was terrible, Bob recovered enough to return to television, although his duties were pared down to match the loss of cognition he continued to experience.

Lee Woodruff's story was inspiring. Angela was all ears. I took notes as fast as I could write. Afterwards, we spoke briefly with her. Angela committed to staying in touch with her from time to time. She has kept that promise and follows the work of the Bob Woodruff Foundation which is dedicated to raising awareness and educating the public about the brain injured and traumatized members of our military. This non-profit foundation has raised millions of dollars for injured veterans and their families.

Angela returned from the late October meeting in Raleigh inspired by what she had learned there. She wanted to put it to use and to test herself.

For a year, she had been living with her dad's family since October 17, 2008. Her time was beginning to drag. Her reasons for being in North Carolina had been whittled down to working with some therapy professionals; those services were readily available in New York.

Mair had moved on to pursue her PhD, but the home was still crowded. The daytime hours found Angela alone with her phone and computer. The weather was restricting her schedule. The mountains experienced a particularly snowy and cold winter. For the first time in years, several inches of snow were on the ground from Thanksgiving on. More snow fell each Friday causing the cancellation of a few of her weekend outings. Nobody could drive up the mountain in the ice and snow to get her. For her to slip and fall on the ice could have been a disaster. She spent the winter getting little exercise and completing a few wrap-up therapy sessions.

10

Moving Back Home to NYC

When March arrived, Angela was ready to leave North Carolina. Keeping her here would have been like holding back a horse wanting to get out of the barn. It can be done by pulling hard on the reins but is sometimes not the right thing to do. This was one of those times.

The North Carolina recovery time had gone well. A lot of progress was evident to all those in contact with Angela. She had worked hard and managed her recovery team effectively.

Staying at her dad's home was beginning to be difficult for all those living there. Charlie had to have grown tired of driving Angela to all her frequent therapy sessions and occasional social events. He never complained but Angela felt he would have been justified if he had.

As the weeks passed, Angela grew tired of waiting around. She was stuck on the mountain in Laurel Park with only her scheduled appointments to look forward to.

199

With everyone gone through the day, she had only the dogs for company. She filled some of the time cleaning the crowded home; she was a considerate guest. But she yearned for her New York City life.

Angela had promised herself she would return to Manhattan "when I am able to do it without being a burden to those around me." As she contemplated her move she considered all the available evidence to assess her readiness. She talked to her therapists and to family members. Did they think she was ready? What would she have to be prepared to do upon her return? Could she survive the rigors of city life? The answers were a mix of encouragement and caution. She determined to return and try it out to see how she did.

Finally, Angela contacted friends in the city and asked about possible living arrangements. A shared apartment would be just great. Understandably she received few responses to her inquiry. Friends are willing to do many things and they already had. However, giving up space in a small apartment to a woman with a brain injury and her dog was asking a lot. Her phone did not ring with invitations to share an apartment.

After Angela's second round of emailed inquiries, a wonderful friend, Caren Browning, offered Angela a safe and comfortable place to live. Before doing so, she had consulted with her own therapist about what she was considering doing. Others describe Caren as a real softy. She describes herself as "a bit of a feeling queen" and while she was aware of Angela's great need, this was no time to say yes just to be nice. She did not want to jump into something potentially disruptive to her life without thinking things through. After all, Caren had lived alone in her modest apartment for ten years.

Angela and Caren share a common bond in addition to the fact that they had once worked as colleagues. In September of 2003, Caren suffered a stroke, the result of a tear to the inside lining of a carotid artery which caused a small clot to dislodge and damage areas of her brain. She was initially paralyzed on the right side of her body and could not speak or focus. After three weeks in the hospital and rehabilitation, these symptoms began to reverse themselves. Caren returned to work and functions well as an executive vice president of a New York public relations firm. However, she has had to learn and employ coping mechanisms for some of the cognition challenges that persist even after seven years. Caren uses her computer and other support devices to help her function at her best.

Caren's friendship with Angela had started back at Hunter PR when both worked there. Their common interests revolved around their work and the full enjoyment of life. They shared a love of good restaurants and good wine. After her stroke, Angela would visit her in the hospital when she could. Caren later returned to work at Hunter and Angela was her "champion" during that time. She gave Caren encouragement when her confidence needed a boost and the two worked together closely on several client campaigns. After Caren moved on from Hunter she and Angela pledged to stay in touch.

At the time of Angela's crash, Caren was taking a few days of rest and relaxation at Rehobeth Beach, Delaware. When a phone call informed her of Angela's severe injuries, she headed back to the city a day earlier than planned. It was time for her to be a champion for Angela. It was her turn.

She went to Westchester Medical Center a couple of times but knew those visits were more symbolic than helpful to Angela, still deeply in a coma. She also made weekend visits with former colleagues to Helen Hayes Rehabilitation Hospital as Angela's recovery progressed. She could tell that having friends there seemed to lift Angela's spirits. Caren knew that Angela's mom was running up big expenses and needed a trip or two back to her own home in Florida. Caren gave her a Jet Blue gift card that she had received as a gift.

Caren said that the more she thought about Angela's request for living arrangements the more she realized that she wanted to respond positively. She asked herself, "Who is better equipped to do this than I am?" Besides the housing, as a stroke survivor, she had a good sense of what Angela would face and be able to do or not to do. She entered into her hosting with her eyes wide-opened.

She had the available space in a conveniently located building filled with friendly residents. A small room that had served as a home office could be transformed into a second bedroom.

There was some discussion and negotiation about the living arrangements. Angela was invited to stay for one year from the date of her arrival. This was not intended to be a permanent arrangement. Angela wanted it that way too. She hoped and intended to be strong enough in a year to live in her own place. Angela could bring her dog Moses, but he could stay only on weekends because Caren had an elderly cat. During the week, he had to live elsewhere. As an animal lover and former cat owner herself, Angela fully understood and succeeded in arranging for another friend to host her beloved dog during the week.

Because they had worked together and been friends for years, Caren knew that Angela was a neat and organized person. She also recognized that Angela was someone who always had a plan for her life and pursued that plan diligently. Caren is eighteen years older than Angela. She knew Angela would want to live as independently as she could and would pay attention to the agreement they had made about sharing the apartment.

Caren also understood that it was just possible that she, Caren, could learn something from Angela. Neural fatigue and confidence were still an occasional issue for her. Living together, the two could potentially share ideas and methods for improving their individual capabilities. She described Angela as being incredibly considerate of others and "almost pathologically nice." Angela could teach her something about friendship and perhaps help Caren to feel less isolated. There were going to be benefits in living with a TBI survivor who was vigorously pursuing her own recovery.

Angela packed her bags and prepared to leave for New York City. Dad Charlie once again provided the chauffeur service. Angela was somewhat apprehensive because if this living arrangement did not work there was no back-up plan. Where could she live if not in Manhattan? It seemed to Angela that she had to make it work. She had no plan B.

Moving into Caren's apartment was easy as Angela brought no furnishings. Her clothing and personal possessions filled a rented SUV. She hoped Caren would not complain as the small apartment filled up.

Caren works all day so Angela had the apartment to herself until the evening. Time alone gave Angela an opportunity to test her independent living skills and to practice her new eye and vestibular exercises. Her iPhone organizer prompted her about what needed doing and when to do it. The challenge was to actually get it done. The device called constantly to "get to your next therapy session, pay your bills, take your medication, eat a meal." The device was helpful even when the frequent reminders sounded off in the middle of something else she was doing. Angela was so thankful for the help provided by her iPhone that she wrote a comprehensive, feature by feature, thank you letter to Apple, the company that designed and sells it. She wanted the company to alert other brain injured people about its potential value in their lives.

Some tasks were made more difficult by the uncertainty of reliable cognitive skills. After weeks of using the kitchen range to cook, she finally admitted that her occupational therapist was right. She had difficulty remembering to turn off the range when finished. The safety issue meant she had to do all her cooking in the microwave oven. That led to the use of many more pre-packaged, microwaveable meals. That solution was less than perfect because of the nutritional implications. Pre-packed meals often contain excessive salt, fat, preservatives and more calories than she needed. This was yet another compromise that a person recovering from a TBI must make in order to attain a degree of independence.

Many aspects about the city itself did not require her to compromise. She discovered something she had not fully appreciated before her severe injury. For years, she had used public transportation. Trains, subways and buses took her around in the city to business meetings and fun events. She now recognized what public transportation meant to her and to thousands of people with various handicaps including the blind, deaf and those confined to wheelchairs.

For her, the use of public transportation was no longer simply an option; it had become a must. With her double vision and cognition issues she could not drive. Public transit meant she could get where she needed to go and do so safely. She could largely avoid the expense of cabs.

She also came to appreciate Manhattan's public parks. She found a couple of small ones close to the shared apartment, pleasant places where she could sit and relax. Often those parks would host a free concert, movie or some other form of entertainment. Angela could have some fun away from the apartment without spending too much of her limited money.

Manhattan became a different place for her. Before her TBI, it had been her workplace and her playground, a place to go out to dinner and a show or big event. After her return, she discovered that it was a warm and friendly hometown that allowed one to live at a slower pace. Her discovery may surprise those who have never needed to recognize and adapt to New York City's slower and quieter side. She reinvented the city to fit her needs and she was thriving there.

Many of her city friends were at Hunter PR. While she expected to maintain those friendships, she knew they would not be the day to day variety she had while working there. She accepted the reality of the change. Knowing is one thing but truly accepting changes forced upon one by something like a TBI can be difficult. Making new friends was on her "to do" list.

Within weeks of her return, her daily schedule began to fill up nicely. She had recovery team appointments, brain-injury support groups, advocacy activities, church and social time with her new friends. Her daily schedule included playing the brain-stimulation games on www.Lumosity.com. She used stimulating programs to keep her brain moving and to record her progress. She hired a personal trainer to help get her body moving again. Not a spectator wishing and hoping for recovery to occur, she is the active boss.

Here is one example of how she did what she did. She joined a brain injury support group that operates out of the State University of New York (SUNY). After her first meeting she realized her recovery had been more successful and complete than it had been for some members of the group. As she had done in North Carolina, she determined that she could be a source of help and reassurance to its members. Her personal gain would be in the gift she was giving.

This brain injury support group was comprised of about fifty people of all ages who displayed a full range of injury consequences. They met monthly to discuss living life with a brain injury and to share ideas about how to help recovery happen. Angela saw that many members felt lonely and isolated. They had little going on between these monthly meetings where the topic always had to do with traumatic brain injury. They craved some social activities.

For whatever reason, the professional coordinator who conducted the meetings had not yet recognized or at least had not responded to their need. Angela stepped forward and asked the group to join her for a free movie night at the famous Bryant Park, just across from SUNY. The movie was the classic James Bond movie, *Goldfinger.*

Angela went to the park well ahead of the scheduled show time. She laid blankets out and floated several red helium-filled balloons so people could find her in the park that evening. Twelve people turned out and all had a good time. After the event, Angela spoke to the professional coordinator of the group. She reported the event's success and explained that as a TBI survivor she could not organize all the future events. She told the coordinator that the survivors really needed outlets like these. Angela is persistent. She will prevail to the benefit of her brain injury survivor group.

Being in Manhattan meant that she had to recruit a third medical and rehabilitation team. Her stay at Helen

Hayes had been 100% about rehabilitation. In North Carolina the rehabilitation schedule had been a little more forgiving, filling about 60% of her weekly schedule. She needed to connect with new therapists and build a weekly schedule. Time was important. She did not want to lose ground or momentum in her recovery.

Unfortunately, "the system" pays less attention to a brain injured person who has been in recovery for more than a year. That may happen because there is such a crush of more recently injured people who need therapy. Also, "the system" needs money to keep going. Many brain injury survivors are financially depleted. Insurance coverage, if there was any, may have been consumed or expired and personal funds have often dried up. Staying in "the system" is a major challenge. Angela managed to stay in the system. Her case attracted the right blend of doctors and therapists. Some of them worked with her at reduced rates or even for free. They liked her and that certainly helped. Being likeable can help a recovering brain injured person stay connected to resources.

Rehabilitation had become a lesser part of her weekly schedule but it was vitally important and the sessions were intense.

When she was not in a scheduled rehab session or doing the homework assigned to her, she had time for a few social engagements and more preparation for her future involvement as an advocate for brain injured people. After more than a year in intense therapies and corrective surgeries, it was time to lead a balanced life. She appreciated having time and enough energy to pursue other interests and activities.

She continued making decisions about her mix of therapies and therapists. She had spent countless hours in therapy sessions and considerable money for those sessions after her insurance ran out. All her living expenses were paid for from a single meager source – her disability check. Something had to give.

Angela concluded that she was no longer benefitting as much from traditional therapies as she once had. She looked for leading edge therapies on a schedule and budget she could manage, and she found them in New York City at Rusk Institute of Rehabilitation Medicine.

Rusk Institute is a national leader and provider of a full range of leading edge therapies. The program that Angela sought help from is directed by Steven Flanagan, MD, a nationally recognized innovator. In a telephone interview with the doctor, I was impressed by his spirit. He battles on behalf of traumatic brain injury survivors every day. He said that fight is more difficult beyond the twenty-fourth month of recovery because, as stated earlier, "the system" tries to pull services away while the survivor tries to stay attached and move forward.

Dr. Flanagan stated quite clearly that a TBI is an event—*not* a chronic disease. That is an important differentiation because a chronic disease is likely to have to be treated and controlled forever; significant improvement or eradication may not be possible. That is not the case with TBI. Making that point with all those who need to understand it, including the TBI survivor, is a part of the fight he wages.

The demands on his time mean he can meet with individual patients only about once a month. His daily efforts are better described as directing an inter-disciplinary team and not a multiple disciplinary team. What is the difference? An inter-disciplinary team works on behalf of the patient without accounting for which therapy gets the most time or attention. Success is shared and is measured by how many patients show marked improvement from their combined team efforts. Dr. Flanagan and others leaders at Rusk Institute of Rehabilitation Medicine have successfully built inter-disciplinary teams. Their clients are the beneficiaries.

Angela decided to concentrate her therapy time and limited funds on vestibular therapy and cognitive remediation sessions. The website www.vestibular.org says that "vestibular rehabilitation therapy (VRT) is an exercise-based program designed to promote central nervous system compensation for inner ear deficits". The recovering TBI is constantly faced with making adjustments in life—forever compensating.

One of Angela's therapists was senior physical therapist, Jennifer Kelly. Nearing two years since the injury, Angela's biggest need was to avoid falls brought on by dizziness, double vision, compromised depth perception and loss of balance. She had fallen a couple of times, once when getting off a bus and once when walking down the stairs at the subway station. Curbs were challenging too. The last thing a brain injured person needs is another fall.

It is not uncommon for head trauma survivors, like Angela, to have something called BPPV or "benign paroxysmal positional vertigo." The room spins with changes in position like bending, reaching, and getting into or out of bed.

Calcium carbonate found in the inner ear becomes detached by a blunt force trauma and moves to another part of the inner ear. BPPV therapy involves exercises that attempt to reposition these calcium crystals within the inner ear. Jennifer worked with her using vestibular therapy exercises.

BPPV can be diagnosed using infrared goggles in which eye movements are projected onto a flat screen to determine exactly where the problem is in the inner ear. The patient wearing the goggles is put through different head positions to recreate the symptoms. The treatment for BPPV is quick and easy and sometimes yields immediate results. Angela was not willing to simply live with dizziness and balance problems. She has benefitted from the treatments but is not yet completely free of symptoms.

Jennifer frequently sees patients in the vestibular therapy lab years after their TBI. The longer the dizziness and balance problems persist the more difficult it can be to tease out what can be corrected and what must simply be compensated for by the survivor. Often therapy "rest sessions" are scheduled during which the TBI is given home practice exercises. Then the survivor returns for more therapy. Those with a TBI can take three times as long to recover as someone with other non-TBI reasons for their dizziness. Patience is called for on the part of both the brain injured person and the therapist. The brain sets its own schedule for neuro-plastic healing and it cannot be rushed.

Angela knew she also needed cognitive remediation. Typically, that calls for the services of a neuropsychologist. She still had attention and memory problems. Some of those, like failing to turn off the range when cooking, could have dire consequences for her. What is cognitive remediation and where would a TBI survivor go to get it? According to the website www.mindisorders.com it is "a teaching process that targets areas of neuropsychological functioning involved in learning and day to day functioning." The expectation is to "bolster specific cognition capacities that are weak and to teach compensatory strategies." Angela describes it as learning how to use your brain again. The issue is compensation versus cure or complete elimination of the problem.

Angela does not complain about having to compensate to get along. She willingly compensates and enjoys the benefits that come with being open to more of it if needed. Of course, we all compensate more than we realize. The need to do it comes naturally as we age and as health problems arise. It comes on us gradually and almost without our noticing that it is happening. But for a person who has suffered a TBI, the need to compensate arrives suddenly and is much easier to identify. The TBI survivor and all those around that person know things have changed and that adjustments must be made.

Angela's post-injury life will always include a few hours each month for rehabilitation of one type or another. She expects that and will gladly do the work required in those sessions. Future therapy will be somewhat like checking the spark plugs and wires in the engine of a car. Her brain will continue to replace and reconnect a neuron here and there to provide for smoother performance.

11

Climbing More Mountains

Two years have passed since Angela's first life ended. At that time it seemed to those around her that it had ended tragically. All that could be counted in those early days were the losses. Lost were her husband of less than one year, a job she loved with a wonderful company, her income and that of her husband, her healthcare benefits, her newly acquired home, and much of her health and strength.

In the summer of 2010 Angela was busy planning a celebration of Rich's life. After being in a coma during his funeral, she had wanted to conduct this celebration. Two years into recovery, she finally has the emotional strength to do it.

As she was planning the event, her friends at Hunter asked her to come and claim the old personal files that they had stored for her. She was curious to see what was there. Here is how she put it in an email to me.

"I didn't remember why I was making a three ring binder that organized the invitations, RSVPs, prayers and catering for Rich's life celebration until Hunter Public Relations asked me to clean out my desk belongings that had been placed in storage. I naively brought a backpack to carry what turned out to be twelve shelves filled with boxes. So that's what eight years looks like? There was a binder for every event I ever hosted, including my wedding and a client's national cook-off championship that I had planned a month before the accident." In the assorted files was a binder of her wedding planning that Angela's mother had returned to her.

How important it must be to her to know that a significant life skill like being organized was not lost to her brain injury. With her ongoing loss of cognition, staying organized will be an asset. For example, keeping personal items in the same place within her apartment will save her time and frustration. She and those around her take pleasure in her retention of pre-TBI living skills that will help her in the future.

Her family, friends, co-workers, neighbors, doctors, nurses and therapists could not be blamed if most of what they saw in those early days/ weeks/ months were her losses. The losses were real but they were not the whole story.

Angela did not spend time recording a list of losses and discussing them. She was too busy struggling to recover and move on. She did not see her life as others seemed to see it. She asked a challenging question: "How many people do you know who get a fresh start in life? This is my second chance. I get a do-over and all things are possible." This is a powerful statement of her acceptance of her new life. Being near her, listening to what she says, watching what she does and understanding how she thinks serves as a reality challenge to all who hear her words and watch her live them.

She had survived and with the fight she began to wage in the earliest days, she ultimately reset the expectations of those around her. Early on, while still in a dramatically vulnerable and weakened condition, she was already charting a new course. Those around her had no way of knowing where this new course would take her, what part they would play, and how their helping her would change their lives.

To look at her and talk with her today you would not know what she has been thorough. Just two years ago she experienced her first helicopter ride—to the trauma center. She knew nothing of that flight. Since then she has taken another helicopter ride; this second one was over the Hoover Dam and the Grand Canyon while on a vacation trip to Las Vegas. What a difference two years of dedicated daily effort have made.

Make no mistake, Angela is not who she once was. There remain issues that are now difficult if not impossible for her to manage. Cooking is one ongoing and perhaps permanent loss in her life. Being able to cook, even for those who choose not to cook, is something most of us take for granted.

Angela was a good cook. She loved planning and preparing an appetizing meal for herself and her friends. Seeing them enjoy the meal was her pay-off. A music-filled evening with good food, good wine and conversation made her happy. Since the brain injury she has discovered (more than once) that she finished cooking but forgot to turn off the burner on the stove. Her rude reminder was the piercing sound of the smoke detector. Angela has given up cooking. Her doctors have also reminded her that brain injured people who use alcohol regularly do so at their own peril. She has given that up as well. She may have just a small glass of wine on special occasions.

Is it possible that Angela is living a more significant life now than she was before the crash that changed so much for her? Prior to the brain injury, Angela was a public relations professional and she did her job well. Now she has become an advocate for others who have suffered brain injuries. She has become a source of inspiration. She regards herself as a soldier in basic training for this role. As she gains experience as an advocate, she will do this job well.

Advocacy for any worthy cause is among the highest order of career challenges. She will often face a public that would rather avoid this difficult topic. When she is involved and energized they will not be able to turn away. She will successfully make the case for needed research and funding.

She will support individuals who have suffered brain injuries. At times, they may expect or even demand too much individual attention to their specific case. Her big heart may mean Angela has a hard time saying no to individual requests for excessive personal help. Some brain injured persons can be very needy and unintentionally demanding of the time of others. She will have to monitor the use of her time so she can work effectively with scores of brain injured people and their recovery teams.

When Angela granted my request to write her story, she presented me with an opportunity to learn what life is really all about. In being close to her and recording her journey, I received more than bargained for and have her to thank. Having just retired, I was on the back side of my own life. Some might suggest that people my age already know more than enough to get through their remaining years. They might suggest coasting to the finish line. I respectfully disagree.

Now, after two years spent in interviews, research and writing, what I learned and from whom I learned it is clear. For those who may already know or one day come to know a brain injured person, please consider what a brain injury survivor has to offer you in exchange for your friendship and support. Believe me, they will give you far more than you can ever give to them.

I learned a great deal from her doctors, nurses, therapists, family and friends—information helpful as background. All of them deserve much thanks for taking the time to provide both information and inspiration. It was also helpful to read books about the brain and other books by those who were writing about their own brain injuries. But it was the time spent with Angela that taught me the most about the reality of brain trauma and all the losses to those who suffer them.

Here are a few lessons about life that my involvement with Angela taught me. Some of these lessons are obvious and perhaps I should already have learned them along life's highway. Yet there are levels of learning that we can all go through. The first and easiest learning is intellectual learning—things we know because we read about them. There is no real emotional investment in intellectual learning.

A far deeper level of learning takes place when you are drawn into a situation that you might easily have justified avoiding. When I chose to get close to Angela, my learning went from the intellect to the gut. At that level, I could begin to understand her pain and suffering.

After starting out as total strangers, I have a true friendship with and deep respect for Angela. From her I have learned:

1) Everything of consequence in one's life can be gone in an instant. Health, well-being, loved ones, job, money and home can all be lost.

2) The will to live may be all that remains. Without that will no one can thrive and may not survive.

3) Good people are all around ready to do whatever it takes to help an injured survivor recover. Many are complete strangers. It is crucial to welcome them and keep them close.

4) Recovery from a significant injury cannot be rushed. It occurs one slow step at a time over several years. If the survivor's attitude is negative and the

necessary dedication to the work required slackens, recovery will slow and then stop.

5) As complete as one's recovery may turn out to be, there will be changes. After a severe brain injury, there may not be a full "return to normal" whatever "normal" may mean.

There are fresh ways to think about normal. Just what is normal and how might we benefit by having a more flexible and adaptable view of it?

All the things that define your state of normality are not the same as the norm for anyone else. Even identical birth twins have different norms. We are all unique and different. As a person grows and ages, one's own "normal" begins to change. Change precedes growth. What was normal at age ten is far from normal for that same person at age thirty. Conditions change and we need to change with them.

Angela never spoke of returning to normal. Her objective was to recover well enough to lead a new and constructive life, a life she viewed as being full of new opportunities yet to be discovered.

In fact, Angela and I have had a lot of laughs about how she is not "normal." Sometimes she cannot recall something and flashes a momentary frustration. At those times I say, "Angela, what do you expect? After all you have had a brain injury and are not normal." She gets it and laughs her reassured laugh. She is as "normal" as I am, as "normal" as any of us. Angela has come to loathe the word.

In truth, we shared some tears—tears of joy. At times some act of kindness was more than anyone could anticipate or easily accept, almost overwhelming. People spoke words of kindness and encouragement to her just at the right time. When those positive and unexpected things happened, joy-filled tears were an expected and accepted reaction.

To accomplish her recovery objectives Angela has had to explore new frontiers and be persistent. She had to be tough and brave. She had to take chances but not crazy risks. She tried new therapies to see if they might work for her. She had to be fully involved with the direction of her treatments. When something was not working she decisively moved on.

There is nothing better for anyone who has have suffered any serious brain insult, from a stroke to a head trauma, than to be fully engaged and creative in the pursuit of healing. Sitting down and waiting for the brain to heal is like sitting down and waiting to lose weight. It cannot work.

Angela is a great accommodator and compensator. It is not easy for her to recall her daily schedule, avoid making conflicting commitments or say no to some requests for her help. Angela gets along well by using newly acquired tools, investing extra time and effort. The key is in accommodation and compensation.

She will likely always have some double vision. The prospects are limited for driving a car or doing other things that require fast refocusing of her eyes. So what has she done to compensate for this loss? She has mastered the use of public transportation in the city. Because she cannot read for extended periods she uses audio books. In fact, she cannot easily read this book about her. She adjusts to these realities.

She has lost many of her life's most precious memories. She does not fret about those losses or dwell in the past. She is too busy making new memories.

Also gone are many of her cognitive skills. In their place, she has her iPhone programmed to "remind" her of appointments and to lock the doors as she leaves for those appointments. She keeps a daily written log of her "mistakes" and seeks ways to compensate for and correct them.

Her former physical strength and stamina are lessened. There are some balance problems too. She must avoid standing on a ladder to reach an item on the top shelf. However, she does not plan on climbing the Rocky Mountains. Instead, she has new mountains to climb and she will.

Along the way, my advice to her was always framed in terms of options or ways to think about things. It was not right or helpful to tell her what she ought to do.

It was difficult to stick strictly to my writing tasks; not content to remain the silent secretary. At times, it was difficult seeing the well-meaning around her not doing for her the things she needed most.

Personal or professional advice was sometimes lacking in its soundness. For example, she continued to pay her mortgage for many months from her meager resources. The realtors failed to obtain a short sale and the bankers forced a foreclosure. In her situation they could have moved to expedite the situation and preserve some of limited cash. They did not act with her in mind. Angela lost her home and her credit rating suffered.

At other times, when she needed to figure something out on her own, people jumped in and tried to fix the problem for her. Those who jumped too soon could have restrained themselves and waited for her to ask. For her safety, they could have observed her as she cross the street but not grabbed her elbow to take her across. That is a subtle but important difference.

My role left me feeling like a combination of author, guardian and counselor. Angela, if I over-did it I apologize.

Along the way I also learned some things that Angela is not. First and foremost, Angela is not a victim. To qualify as a victim, one must submit to the pain and suffering. She did not allow her pain and suffering to make her their victim. She did not deny; she dealt. Victimhood has a cunning and subtle appeal. Fortunately, it did not appeal to Angela.

Neither is she some kind of hero. To be a hero one must make a decision and act upon that decision. Think of the military soldier who makes a split-second decision to jump on a hand grenade to save the lives of comrades. Angela did not decide to sustain severe physical injuries and a brain scramble; thus she is not a hero. (Refreshingly, she will tell you the same thing.) Many traits do make her a treasure. She is a strong person, a wonderful role model, a great friend, and an effective advocate for brain injured persons. But all of those do not make her a hero.

Finally, she is not one of a kind, not the rare exception. We met many people who have suffered

228

severe brain injuries and committed to doing the hard and never-ending work required to recover. They have made marvelous progress and many are willing, even eager, to share their success stories. Angela is inspirational, but she is not a singular exception; not the only brain injured person who is succeeding in life.

Her second life vaguely resembles her first life. She has adjusted and life is improving – not easy but better. Most of the intense medical interventions, painful operations and therapy sessions are behind her. However, there will always be after-effects.

The early, intense and grueling interventions have now been replaced by a regular and routine set of therapies appropriate at this stage of her post injury life. Angela spoke with her physician one year after she began the use of the medications he had prescribed. She had been told their use would help her avoid short periods of sadness or depression. She realized that smoothing highs and lows with drugs was not for her. Life before her brain injury included highs and lows, but on anti-depressants she felt numb. She had lived with highs and lows in the past and decided she would do so again. She decided to first cut down and then eliminate their use. Living an emotionally flattened life was not for Angela.

Of course, complete withdrawal from the use of medications is not always an option for a brain injured person. In fact, Angela may, from time to time in the future, resume the use of medications if she and her doctors think it makes sense to deal with some issue. Using drugs that truly help is advisable. Using them to zone out and stay that way is dangerous.

Since discontinuing the use of mood-modifying, anti-depressant drugs and with additional healing time her brain needed, she has discovered that some memories do make her sad. Some returning memories bring tears to her eyes. For example, when the bank foreclosed on her home, she had one month to remove all of her possessions. A couple of her friends were there to help. All was going smoothly as they opened cartons to survey their contents. When Angela opened boxes containing baby clothes, she broke down and cried. She had forgotten about those clothes, given to her by her sister-in-law Denise. Being suddenly and forcefully reminded that she and Rich had planned to have children was just too much. For a brain injury survivor, tears can indicate emotional healing.

"Settled in" might best describe Angela's new life. She is settled into a daily schedule that matches her capabilities while providing stimulation and challenge.

Getting "settled in" is a good thing. Her family and friends can stop wondering every day how she is doing and whether she is okay. We know that she is okay and that she will reach out for help if one day she discovers that she is not. All those who care about her can rest with that reassurance.

All books must end. As we wrap this one up I cannot avoid some conjecture about where life may take her. Angela is a determined fighter so I tend to believe upbeat conjectures concerning her future are more likely than the downbeat ones.

As you look at these conjectures, you need to know that before Angela ever heard a word written in this book, I shared with her a major concern. Its honesty could make her uncomfortable. If she could handle the emotional discomfort of having her story truthfully told, there could be a second level of discomfort for her. How might readers, especially those in the brain injured community, feel about what was shared on its pages? What might they think of her after reading it? After we discussed these concerns, she assured me that she was unafraid and ready to go full speed ahead.

Here are my downbeat conjectures.

Angela suffered horrific physical and brain injuries. A body so critically injured cannot be expected to be as good as new. She will have to be selective about her activities: riding a bicycle, jogging, skating, using a ladder, skiing or hiking difficult terrain are out. Another blow to the head could be devastating and life threatening.

Her severely broken shoulder could become immobile and arthritic in the future, but ongoing physical therapy may forestall that problem.

It would be unrealistic to expect a physically active and pain-free life for her because of how badly broken her body was in the crash. In fact, shoulder, neck and back pain seem likely in future years.

She may experience more loss of brain function earlier than had she never suffered the brain injury. Those whose earlier lives included a brain injury tend to experience earlier onset of some difficult cognition problems and dementia.

Her life may include emotional pain as well. She may find herself more often operating alone than she would have been as a public relations executive.

Those friends who knew her before the brain injury may never perceive her to be recovered enough to establish a full and trusting relationship with her. When friends have issues with Angela an honest discussion should resolve them. How unfair and unreal would her life be if everyone around her tried so hard to be nice that they avoided those discussions or avoided her altogether. Angela and most brain injured people are capable of and want full relationships. They should not be treated as lesser beings in our lives. In some ways they are stronger and more worth knowing than those so-called "normal" people among us.

She may have difficulty finding a loving marital partner. Upon discovery of her history, a new man may regard her as damaged and not worth the risk. Or a man may stay because he pities her. Relationships are never easy and hers most assuredly won't be an exception.

Permit me to offer some positive conjectures about her future. Given the type of person she is, the upsides seem to be more likely. Here are a few of them.

Those around her will begin to deal with her as Angela and not as "poor, brain-injured Angela." Their acceptance is important. She does not want her friends and acquaintances to be forever stuck in sympathy and pity while she is happily moving on with her life. If they over-do the pity she will call them on it.

She will likely continue to attract and retain friends and followers. She will be a beacon for those living with brain injuries and for those involved with them. She will be an inspiration to thousands of people she will never personally meet.

She will observe and enjoy things around her. A slower pace will make a simple' walk in the park a real joy. A good meal will bring enjoyment. She loves music and her singing voice will return to the strength it once had.

She will make healthy choices concerning nutrition and regular exercise. She will be moderate in the consumption of wine or abstain completely. Concentrating on nutrition and exercise, she will feel better and set a good example for others.

She will work again diligently and effectively in a field that suites her needs and capabilities, likely as an advocate for brain injured people but not necessarily limited to that field.

Finally, she will meet someone who will love her for all the right reasons. She has so much love to give.

I believe positive things await her. In a few years, we will know what good things have happened. From everything I have seen in these first two years, we can all expect great things.

The end of this book marks the beginning of Angela's second life. She is back home in Manhattan and loving her life there. From there she will write additional, compelling chapters. For now, it is only fitting that

Angela's words conclude the last chapter of this first book. Here they are:

"There is a hardworking guardian angel who makes this journey bearable and there isn't a day that goes by that I haven't felt Rich at my side. Sometimes his presence is made obvious through songs that happen to play around me, like the time his favorite Del Amitri song came on the satellite radio while I was strapped into a treadmill at physical therapy. I later discovered the obscure song Tell Her on my laptop under music Rich uploaded onto my computer. There's occasionally a subtle sensation of knowing I'm not alone in a room when standing there by myself.

And yet, I cannot remember him.

My doctor explained that one-year before and one-year after the accident creates a two-year amnesiac window and it is possible that I won't recall those memories. Rich and I got married within that window. I've seen lovely wedding and honeymoon photos where the bride and groom appear blissful, but I cannot recall the emotions associated with those images. I cannot recall what it felt like when he placed the band of diamonds on my finger. I mustered the courage to remove my wedding ring from my left hand and now wear it on a chain near my heart. My finger still bears the indentation and I want desperately to remember what it felt like the first time I put it on.

I believe Rich has my recovery all under control, and knows that I'd have a harder and slower time of it with a broken heart. When he thinks I'm ready, I know he will know and tell me so.

I have finally laid down the enormous guilt of being a widow who feels no sadness. A year and a half passed without me being able to shed so much as a single tear for my dead husband. You cannot imagine the shame I felt whenever someone's expression revealed more sadness for me than I felt in my own heart. Tears never wet my cheeks and I could not understand why. I now understand it is the brain's way of protecting me from experiencing overwhelming emotions, which explains why people often feel "numb" after tragedies.

But things are changing—I'm starting to feel more alive, returning to my skin and experiencing the fullness of my situation. And yes, now that even includes tears. A support group for brain injury survivors meets monthly and always opens with introductions. For the first time, when I offered the "canned" intro, that I'd rehearsed as much for my own benefit as others, I felt a frog growing in my throat, my heart raced and I sensed other survivors shifting nervously as my voice cracked.

Being on Lexapro for a period after the accident raised my lows but suppressed my highs, making my emotions as flat as a pancake. I've decided if an unbearable tidal wave of sadness comes crashing onto my soul's shore, I'll willingly return to the "chemical numbness" of an anti-depressant. For now, however, I'm finally remembering what it feels like to be sad and I'm okay with that. Sadness is an appropriate emotion for a thirty-year-old widow coming to grips with the recent loss of her soul mate.

Perhaps the most frustrating part of this recovery, more than having to relearn to walk and write, is losing two fundamental parts of my being, parts that helped tell my story and define me as a person; singing and dancing. I realize this may sound vain, but if you ever joined me in a karaoke bar or dance club before August of 2008, you would understand.

Dancing was cemented in my character after long college nights spent on countless dance floors. Because I was too young to drink, I found the best way to pass time was by making my way onto the floor. I had always been a person who sought attention, but never on a dance floor. My movements were the purest form of self-expression and never for anyone else. I often forgot that there was anyone else on the dance floor besides the music and me. I'd feel rhythm from a place deep down inside.

My balance and coordination are so challenged now that I can no longer walk in a straight line or stand on one leg. I've taken terrible falls off buses, and I sometimes accidentally walk into oncoming traffic. I can clap out a beat with my hands but cannot translate that beat to my body. It pains me to consider the difference between what it once was, and the way things are today.

Since I was a small child in the church choir, singing has been a staple of my life. I grew up singing with Daddy as he played guitar. My husband was a talented musician and he recorded me harmonizing on several of his tracks. Several karaoke bars in Manhattan knew me by name. In fact, karaoke was a bonding strategy I used with clients on business trips. I've been singing for as long as I can remember. It's engrained in who I am—it's part of my identity. The trauma of a tracheotomy has taken my singing voice temporarily. I guess it's a fair tradeoff to have a hole stabbed through my throat in order to breathe.

When someone loses a person they love, that loss is clear and there is something tangible to grieve. In many ways, it is easier to grieve a death than it is to lose a part of yourself. The reality is I've lost more than a *young husband, a career and lifestyle. I'd venture to guess that this loss of self is the most upsetting loss for most traumatic brain injury survivors. We're all trying to figure out how to live as a different person. How do we accept our new selves and gain the acceptance of others as this new person? We've lost so much of who we were and are approaching our lives as if on training wheels.*

And yet, these losses do not have to mean the end of the world. I quickly broke the habit of referring to myself in the past tense or "the old me" because I didn't like how that sounded or felt. Returning to the "old me" would be taking steps backwards. So I began focusing on the new me.

Here's my unsolicited advice to all traumatic brain injury survivors: don't idly sit back and watch your recovery pass you by. Yes, there are paid professionals who work with you and provide you with their expertise, but this is only the beginning of your rehabilitation. The real benefit of their labor begins when you commit to doing whatever homework the professionals and therapists recommend. I have a chart of all the exercises I need to complete daily:

1) *Vestibular therapy: 7/8 Romberg eyes open, 1/4 Romberg eyes closed, and a full Romberg for one minute.*

2) *Vision therapy: Brock string exercises, and watch my reflection in a spoon to increase range of motion in my right eye.*

3) *Brain and cognition training with daily sessions on Lumosity.com.*

4) *Physical therapy prescribed exercises to strengthen my knee and my balance.*

I've wondered why my recovery seems to be going so well and I thought maybe it's the type or location of my brain injury. But my former occupational therapist told me that my injuries are significant and not localized. The real payoff is coming because I do what I am told. Sure, there are days when I have to force myself to take out the Brock string or do Rombergs when I would rather nap. But there is an internal flame, or a guardian angel, that gives me reason to work hard. The benefits are becoming obvious and the daily improvement is very fulfilling. I want you to experience this recovery too; it is within every survivor's reach. I encourage you to organize and to be an active player on your recovery team.

During trauma of this magnitude, you have got to be your own greatest advocate. After I regained consciousness, I invited every member of my recovery team to be a player. I identified my weaknesses and asked for help in those specific areas. It takes great courage to know when and where you are weak, and even greater courage to ask for help. This is the key to my continued recovery. I never stop acknowledging and thanking those people for their role and contributions.

If you are not physically, cognitively or emotionally able to be your own quarterback, identify this area of weakness and seek help. This goes for your caregivers too. The refreshing discovery I've had in this journey is that there are plenty of people surrounding us who are willing to help if they are asked.

Every survivor has a story of horrific tragedy. Rather than dwelling on the "how" we got our brain injuries and what we can no longer do as a result, consider what gifts this injury has given you. What can you do now that you could not have done before the accident? For example, these days I cannot multitask. In the past, I always had two, three or ten things on my plate at once. Now when you are talking with me, you get my full and undivided attention. To my benefit and that of those around me, my new ability to provide my undivided attention is a gift.

I also feel as though I have the wisdom of my grandmother trapped inside my young body. I smile when I hear young ladies talk about their new shoes or jeans. I just don't have those concerns anymore. My value system has completely shifted and I see this as one of my gifts.

I shared a realization with my dad; every survivor I meet has such a sad story—divorce, wheelchair-bound, total loss of independence. He mentioned that similar things could be said of my story. Under these circumstances, it is natural for depression to sink in. My heart breaks to sit back and watch my friends all grow their families, during a time when I found my own family shrinking.

This is a perfect time for depression to come knocking on your door. When on disability's schedule, I found the best way to cope with a maddening period of non-productivity and extra time is to book my calendar and stay busy. Real busy. My perspective changed from feeling sorry for myself because no one invites me out anymore, to inviting myself out to reconnect with them. Why should the responsibility be theirs alone? I'm encouraged each time I reach out to someone who I haven't seen in years because they are just ecstatic to be remembered by me. TBI or not, many of us feel alone in the world much more than we'd like. I take this initiative seriously and have been planning reunions at least twice a week. The list has included former associates at Hunter Public Relations, editors I use to work with, my first intern, my junior-year prom date, former clients, and folks from out-of-town who are passing through New York City.

To anyone who's ever been a patient, a survivor, I urge you to take time and thank those who helped you. I refer to these doctors, nurses, paramedics, therapists, psychologists, support groups, family and friends as my recovery team and I make a point of telling them how valuable their contribution is.

That is especially true of your professional medical therapy team members. The nurse on Life Fight Jena Canavan told me, "Thank you so much. It is miracles like you that make our job worth every moment." More often than not, those moments include low salaries, long hours, poor equipment, and difficult client personalities. Many members of my recovery team are greatly underpaid and highly overworked. Be the reason they continue their work. Inspire them to be the miracles that make our lives worth living – literally.

To all those who have touched my life (physically, emotionally, and those I never met but who held me in prayer), I thank you from a place deeper than my heart. The time, talent and money you invested to save and restore my life were not wasted. I refuse to believe that this was an "accident." God is not that cruel. God has a bigger plan and I anticipate the adventure that lies ahead.

I believe in the power of affirmations. Many of you might not venture a guess at the outcome of my story. At the risk of spoiling the surprise, let me tell you the end. I have very clear affirmations of the direction of my life:

1) I will become an effective advocate for traumatic brain injury survivors and their families.

2) I will sing again.

3) I will find the second love of my life."

Acknowledgment

Note from Angela: As Bill read a draft of this manuscript aloud to me for the first time, he stopped several times to clear his throat and get the lumps out. It was then I realized how much writing this book has meant to him. This is more than the emotionally detached recording of a personal history. Bill's emotional response was my first glimpse of what this work and our friendship means to him.

I've grown to consider Bill a trusted advocate, a great driver and a dear friend. These past two years of recovery would not have been the same without his presence in my life. I'm grateful we connected with each other when I wobbled into the public relations association meeting where we first met.

Thank you, Bill, for investing those sleepless nights, for attending the Raleigh conferences with me, for driving me to where I needed to be, for the hours of interviews and research you did, for standing beside me when I visited Rich's grave for the first time, and for listening. Thank you for being you.

Angela Leigh Tucker as told by Bill Ramsey

Appendix

Suggested Books

Brain Rules, John Medina

In an Instant, Lee Woodruff

Brain Injury Survival Kit, Cheryle Sullivan, MD

Mind Storms, Guide for Families Living with TBI, Dr. John W. Cassidy

The Winner's Brain, 8 Strategies Great Minds Use to Achieve Success, Jeff Brown

Helpful Websites

www.TraumaticBrainInjuryatoz.org

www.biausa.org

www.nabis.org

www.BrainLine.org

www.Lumosity.com

www.braininjuryresearchinstitute.org

www.getrealresults.com/tenmyths

www.helenhayeshospital.org

www.bianc.net

www.bianys.org

Angela Leigh Tucker as told by Bill Ramsey

Postscript—October 2013

Angela is now five years into recovery and continues to make progress. Her life has a regularity to it now. She continues her therapy, exercises and is careful about her nutrition. She enjoys good health, is active in her church and advocacy.

Angela understands that many brain-injury survivors may not recover to the extent that she has. The challenges issued in this book are meant to be a positive example for others. The photo below was taken in the lobby of the Helen Hayes Rehabilitation Hospital. Its message applies nicely to all of us, even those fortunate enough to never have suffered a brain injury.

Angela Leigh Tucker as told by Bill Ramsey

Made in the USA
Charleston, SC
10 January 2014